Grade 1

Pearson Scott Foresman

Leveled Reader
Teaching Guide

Glenview, Illinois • Boston, Massachusetts • Chandler, Arizona • Upper Saddle River, New Jersey

ISBN: 13: 978-0-328-48446-1
ISBN: 10:   0-328-48446-6
8 9 10 11 12 V016 15 14 13 12

Table of Contents

LEVELED READER TITLE	Instruction	Comprehension Practice	Vocabulary Practice
Sam	12–13	14	15
Bix the Dog	16–17	18	19
On the Farm	20–21	22	23
Time for Dinner	24–25	26	27
At Your Vet	28–29	30	31
Fun in the Sun	32–33	34	35
We Are a Family	36–37	38	39
The Class Play	40–41	42	43
Here in My Neighborhood	44–45	46	47
Look at Dinosaurs	48–49	50	51
Around the Forest	52–53	54	55
Learn About Worker Bees	56–57	58	59
In My Room	60–61	62	63
Hank's Song	64–65	66	67
Gus the Pup	68–69	70	71
The Seasons Change	72–73	74	75
Animals Change and Grow	76–77	78	79
Ready for Winter?	80–81	82	83

Graphic Organizers

Introduction

Scott Foresman *Reading Street* provides more than 750 leveled readers that help children become better readers and build a lifelong love of reading. The *Reading Street* leveled readers are engaging texts that help children practice critical reading skills and strategies. They also provide opportunities to build vocabulary, understand concepts, and develop reading fluency.

The leveled readers were developed to be age-appropriate and appealing to children at each grade level. The leveled readers consist of engaging texts in a variety of genres, including fantasy, folk tales, realistic fiction, historical fiction, and narrative and expository nonfiction. To better address real-life reading skills that children will encounter in testing situations and beyond, a higher percentage of nonfiction texts is provided at each grade.

USING THE LEVELED READERS

You can use the leveled readers to meet the diverse needs of your children. Consider using the readers to

- practice critical skills and strategies
- build fluency
- build vocabulary and concepts
- build background for the main selections in the student book
- provide a variety of reading experiences, e.g., shared, group, individual, take-home, readers' theater

GUIDED READING APPROACH

The *Reading Street* leveled readers are leveled according to Guided Reading criteria by experts trained in Guided Reading. The Guided Reading levels increase in difficulty within a grade level and across grade levels. In addition to leveling according to Guided Reading criteria, the instruction provided in the *Leveled Reader Teaching Guide* is compatible with Guided Reading instruction. An instructional routine is provided for each leveled reader. This routine is most effective when working with individual children or small groups.

MANAGING THE CLASSROOM

When using the leveled readers with individuals or small groups, you'll want to keep the other children engaged in meaningful, independent learning tasks. Establishing independent practice stations throughout the classroom and child routines for these stations can help you manage the rest of the class while you work with individuals or small groups. Practice stations can include listening, phonics, vocabulary, independent reading, and cross-curricular activities. For classroom management, create a work board that lists the stations and which children should be at each station. Provide instructions at each station that detail the tasks to be accomplished. Update the board and alert children when they should rotate to a new station. For additional support for managing your classroom, see the *Reading Street* Practice Stations' *Classroom Management Handbook*.

USING THE LEVELED READER TEACHING GUIDE

The *Leveled Reader Teaching Guide* provides an instruction plan for each leveled reader based on the same instructional routine.

INTRODUCE THE BOOK The Introduction includes suggestions for creating interest in the text by discussing the title and author, building background, and previewing the book and its features.

READ THE BOOK Before children begin reading the book, have them set purposes for reading and discuss how they can use the reading strategy as they read. Determine how you want children in a particular group to read the text—softly or silently, to a specific point, or the entire text. Then use the Comprehension Questions to provide support as needed and to assess comprehension.

REVISIT THE BOOK The Think and Share questions provide opportunities for children to demonstrate their understanding of the text, the target comprehension skill, and vocabulary. The Response Options require children to revisit the text to respond to what they've read and to move beyond the text to explore related content.

SKILL WORK The Skill Work box provides instruction and practice for the target skill and strategy and selection vocabulary. Instruction for an alternate comprehension skill allows teachers to provide additional skill instruction and practice for children.

USING THE GRAPHIC ORGANIZERS

Graphic organizers in blackline-master format can be found on pages 132–153. These can be used as overhead transparencies or as worksheets.

ASSESSING PERFORMANCE

Use the assessment forms that begin on page 6 to make notes about your children's reading skills, use of reading strategies, and general reading behaviors.

MEASURE FLUENT READING (pp. 6–7) Provides directions for measuring a child's fluency, based on words correct per minute (wcpm), and reading accuracy using a running record.

OBSERVATION CHECKLIST (p. 8) Allows you to note the regularity with which children demonstrate their understanding and use of reading skills and strategies.

READING BEHAVIORS CHECKLIST (p. 9) Provides criteria for monitoring certain reading behaviors.

READING STRATEGY ASSESSMENT (p. 10) Provides criteria for evaluating each child's proficiency as a strategic reader.

PROGRESS REPORT (p. 11) Provides a means to track a child's book-reading progress over a period of time by noting the level at which a child reads and his or her accuracy at that level. Reading the chart from left to right gives you a visual model of how quickly a child is making the transition from one level to the next. Share these reports with parents or guardians to help them see how their child's reading is progressing.

Measure
Fluent Reading

Taking a Running Record

A running record is an assessment of a child's oral reading accuracy and oral reading fluency. Reading accuracy is based on the number of words read correctly. Reading fluency is based on the reading rate (the number of words correct per minute) and the degree to which a child reads with a "natural flow."

How to Measure Reading Accuracy

1. Choose a grade-level text of about 80 to 120 words that is unfamiliar to the child.
2. Make a copy of the text for yourself. Make a copy for the child or have the child read aloud from a book.
3. Give the child the text and have the child read aloud. (You may wish to record the child's reading for later evaluation.)
4. On your copy of the text, mark any miscues or errors the child makes while reading. See the running record sample on page 7, which shows how to identify and mark miscues.
5. Count the total number of words in the text and the total number of errors made by the child. Note: If a child makes the same error more than once, such as mispronouncing the same word multiple times, count it as one error. Self-corrections do not count as actual errors. Use the following formula to calculate the percentage score, or accuracy rate:

$$\frac{\text{Total Number of Words} - \text{Total Number of Errors}}{\text{Total Number of Words}} \times 100 = \text{percentage score}$$

Interpreting the Results

- A child who reads **95–100%** of the words correctly is reading at an **independent level** and may need more challenging text.
- A child who reads **90–94%** of the words correctly is reading at an **instructional level** and will likely benefit from guided instruction.
- A child who reads **89%** or fewer of the words correctly is reading at a **frustrational level** and may benefit most from targeted instruction with lower-level texts and intervention.

How to Measure Reading Rate (WCPM)

1. Follow Steps 1–3 above.
2. Note the exact times when the child begins and finishes reading.
3. Use the following formula to calculate the number of words correct per minute (WCPM):

$$\frac{\text{Total Number of Words Read Correctly}}{\text{Total Number of Seconds}} \times 60 = \text{words correct per minute}$$

Interpreting the Results

By the end of the year, a first-grader should be reading approximately 45–60 WCPM.

Running Record Sample

Running Record Sample

Notations

Beth and her friends were eating   6

(lunch) in the park.   10

"Tell us about your trip to the   17

beach," Beth said to one of her friends.   25

"It was great!" /grēt/ her friend said.   31

Beth's friends talked about sports,   36

and they talked about movies. But Beth   43

was not talking. and She was looking away.   50

"Beth?" they called to her.   55

Beth did not speak. She was looking   62

at bird. It had landed on a sign. Beth   71

just stared. (sc)   73

"I have a feeling," Beth said at last.   81

"What does that mean?" her friends   87

asked.   88

Beth took out her drawing pad. "I H   95

need to draw that bird, " she Beth said.   102

Accurate Reading
The child reads a word correctly.

Omission
The child omits words or word parts.

Mispronunciation/Misreading
The child pronounces or reads a word incorrectly.

Insertion
The child inserts words or parts of words that are not in the text.

Self-correction
The child reads a word incorrectly but then corrects the error. Do not count self-corrections as actual errors. However, noting self-corrections will help you identify words the child finds difficult.

Hesitation
The child hesitates over a word, and the teacher provides the word. Wait several seconds before telling the child what the word is.

Substitution
The child substitutes words or parts of words for the words in the text.

Running Record Results
Total Number of Words: **102**
Number of Errors: **5**

Reading Time: **136 seconds**

▶ **Reading Accuracy**

$$\frac{102 - 5}{102} \times 100 = 95.098 = 95\%$$

Accuracy Percentage Score: **95%**

▶ **Reading Rate—WCPM**

$$\frac{97}{136} \times 60 = 42.794 = 43 \text{ words correct per minute}$$

Reading Rate: **43 WCPM**

Observation Checklist

Child's Name _____ Date _____

Behaviors Observed	Always (Proficient)	Usually (Fluent)	Sometimes (Developing)	Rarely (Novice)

Reading Strategies and Skills

Behaviors Observed	Always (Proficient)	Usually (Fluent)	Sometimes (Developing)	Rarely (Novice)
Uses prior knowledge and preview to understand what book is about				
Makes predictions and checks them while reading				
Uses context clues to figure out meanings of new words				
Uses phonics and syllabication to decode words				
Self-corrects while reading				
Reads at an appropriate reading rate				
Reads with appropriate intonation and stress				
Uses fix-up strategies				
Identifies story elements: character, setting, plot, theme				
Summarizes plot or main ideas accurately				
Uses target comprehension skill to understand the text better				
Responds thoughtfully about the text				

Reading Behaviors and Attitudes

Enjoys listening to stories				
Chooses reading as a free-time activity				
Reads with sustained interest and attention				
Participates in discussion about books				

General Comments

Reading Behaviors Checklist

Child's Name _____ Date _____

Behavior	Yes	No	Not Applicable
Recognizes letters of the alphabet			
Recognizes name in print			
Recognizes some environmental print, such as signs and logos			
Knows the difference between letters and words			
Knows the difference between capital and lowercase letters			
Understands function of capitalization and punctuation			
Recognizes that book parts, such as the cover, title page, and table of contents, offer information			
Recognizes that words are represented in writing by specific sequences of letters			
Recognizes words that rhyme			
Distinguishes rhyming and nonrhyming words			
Knows letter-sound correspondences			
Identifies and isolates initial sounds in words			
Identifies and isolates final sounds in words			
Blends sounds to make spoken words			
Segments one-syllable spoken words into individual phonemes			
Reads consonant blends and digraphs			
Reads and understands endings, such as -es, -ed, -ing			
Reads vowels and vowel diphthongs			
Reads and understands possessives			
Reads and understands compound words			
Reads simple sentences			
Reads simple stories			
Understands simple story structure			
Other:			

Reading Strategy Assessment

Child _____ Date _____

Teacher _____

		Proficient	Developing	Emerging	Not showing trait
Building Background Comments:	Previews	☐	☐	☐	☐
	Asks questions	☐	☐	☐	☐
	Predicts	☐	☐	☐	☐
	Activates prior knowledge	☐	☐	☐	☐
	Sets own purposes for reading	☐	☐	☐	☐
	Other:	☐	☐	☐	☐
Comprehension Comments:	Retells/summarizes	☐	☐	☐	☐
	Questions, evaluates ideas	☐	☐	☐	☐
	Relates to self/other texts	☐	☐	☐	☐
	Paraphrases	☐	☐	☐	☐
	Rereads/reads ahead for meaning	☐	☐	☐	☐
	Visualizes	☐	☐	☐	☐
	Uses decoding strategies	☐	☐	☐	☐
	Uses vocabulary strategies	☐	☐	☐	☐
	Understands key ideas of a text	☐	☐	☐	☐
	Other:	☐	☐	☐	☐
Fluency Comments:	Adjusts reading rate	☐	☐	☐	☐
	Reads for accuracy	☐	☐	☐	☐
	Uses expression	☐	☐	☐	☐
	Other:	☐	☐	☐	☐
Connections Comments:	Relates text to self	☐	☐	☐	☐
	Relates text to text	☐	☐	☐	☐
	Relates text to world	☐	☐	☐	☐
	Other:	☐	☐	☐	☐
Self-Assessment Comments:	Is aware of: Strengths	☐	☐	☐	☐
	Needs	☐	☐	☐	☐
	Improvement/achievement	☐	☐	☐	☐
	Sets and implements learning goals	☐	☐	☐	☐
	Maintains logs, records, portfolio	☐	☐	☐	☐
	Works with others	☐	☐	☐	☐
	Shares ideas and materials	☐	☐	☐	☐
	Other:	☐	☐	☐	☐

Progress Report

Child's Name _____

At the top of the chart, record the book title, its grade/unit/week (for example, 1.2.3), and the child's accuracy percentage. See page 6 for measuring fluency, calculating accuracy and reading rates. At the bottom of the chart, record the date you took the running record. In the middle of the chart, make an X in the box across from the level of the child's reading—frustrational level (below 89% accuracy), instructional level (90–94% accuracy), or independent level (95–100% accuracy). Record the reading rate (WCPM) in the next row.

Book Title						
Grade/Unit/Week						
Reading Accuracy Percentage						
LEVEL — **Frustrational** (89% or below)						
Instructional (90–94%)						
Independent (95% or above)						
Reading Rate (WCPM)						
Date						

Sam

SUMMARY A boy named Jack finds that Sam the duck makes a fine indoor pet.

LESSON VOCABULARY

come	in	my
on	way	

INTRODUCE THE BOOK

INTRODUCE THE TITLE AND AUTHOR Discuss with children the author and title of *Sam*. Explain that the author, Alan Levine, wrote the words and that the illustrator, Phyllis Pollema-Cahill, drew the illustrations. Point out the cover illustration that shows a duck in the bathtub and ask children if they have ever seen a real duck indoors.

BUILD BACKGROUND Involve children in a discussion about ducks. Ask them if they know where ducks usually live. Remind them of songs, stories, and poems they know that relate to ducks. If children have seen ducks, ask them to talk about this experience. Ask children if, based on what they know about ducks, they think a duck would make a good indoor pet. Encourage them to give reasons for their answers.

PREVIEW Invite children to take a picture walk through the book. Read the title page and point out the title and names of the author and illustrator. Explain that this information always appears on this page. Tell children that the boy shown on page 4 is named Jack. Ask them to describe the setting of the scene and what the boy is doing. Turn to page 5 and discuss what Jack is doing in this illustration. On page 6, point out the real duck and the rubber ducky in the bathtub. Ask children to predict how the story might end.

READ THE BOOK

SET PURPOSE Help children set a purpose for reading *Sam*. Model setting a purpose: "From the cover, it looks like this is a story about a duck swimming in a bathtub. That's a really funny idea. I'm going to read more about it." Suggest that children think about the questions and comments that arose as they previewed the illustrations.

STRATEGY SUPPORT: MONITOR AND CLARIFY Suggest that children work in pairs or small groups as they read. Encourage them to think aloud and to ask their classmates questions about the text, story, and illustrations. Model questioning: "I wonder if Jack is taking a bath too. What do you think?"

COMPREHENSION QUESTIONS

PAGE 4 Do you think Sam came with his name, or that Jack named his pet? Why do you think so? *(Responses will vary.)*

PAGE 5 Do you think that Sam can understand Jack when he tells him to go to the tub? Why or why not? *(Possible response: No, ducks don't understand people.)*

PAGE 6 Is the bathtub a good place for a duck? Why or why not? *(Possible response: Yes, because ducks like water.)*

PAGE 7 What do you think Jack is trying to do? *(Possible response: It looks like Jack is trying to feed Sam something.)*

REVISIT THE BOOK

THINK AND SHARE

1. quacks, comes to Jack, swims, eats snacks
2. Jack takes Sam to the tub.
3. *Sam, can, Jack*
4. Responses will vary but may include that Jack has room for a duck.

EXTEND UNDERSTANDING Invite children to discuss the illustrations after they have read the book. Ask: Did the illustrations help you read? Ask volunteers to point out their favorite illustration.

RESPONSE OPTIONS

WRITING Begin a class chart with the predictable sentence pattern *Sam can ___* . Complete the first sentence and then ask each child to suggest a conclusion to the sentence. Write the children's sentences on the chart. Read the chart together. Invite children to copy and illustrate their sentences to make a class book.

MATH CONNECTION

Make a graph to show what kinds of pets children in the class have. List kinds of pets on a chart and have children put a check mark next to the kind of pet they own. Discuss the results: How many pets are there? What kind of pet is there the most of? The least? Does anyone have a duck?

Skill Work

TEACH/REVIEW VOCABULARY

Print the vocabulary words on index cards. Display the cards one at a time and read the words as a group. Then ask children to pretend they are writing each word on a large chalkboard. Have them say each letter as they "write" it in the air. After each word is spelled out, have children say the word as they "erase" it.

ELL Give each child a vocabulary word card, and have children find their word somewhere in the classroom. Encourage children to search other books and in environmental print. Invite them to share their discoveries with their classmates.

TARGET SKILL AND STRATEGY

CHARACTER AND SETTING Explain that characters are people in stories. The setting is where the story takes place. Characters can be real or made up. In *Sam*, the main characters are Sam and Jack. Tell children that when they read, they can think about how characters in a story feel. Ask: When Jack picked Sam as a pet, how do you think he felt? How can you tell?

MONITOR AND CLARIFY Remind children that what they read should make sense. When they encounter a word they don't know, finding out what the word means can help them understand what they read. They can look the word up in the dictionary to find its meaning.

ADDITIONAL SKILL INSTRUCTION

DRAW CONCLUSIONS Point out to children that as they read, they can use what they have read and what they already know about real life to figure out more about the characters and what happens in the story. Model drawing conclusions. Say: "In the beginning of the story, Jack is with some ducks outside. But then we see Sam. And we see that Sam is with Jack inside Jack's house. You usually don't see animals in a house unless they are pets. Sam must be Jack's pet."

Character

1. Show how Jack takes care of Sam. Draw a picture.

2. Would you want Jack to be your friend? (Yes) (No)

_____

- -

_____

Why or why not?

_____

- -

_____

- -

_____

Name_____

Vocabulary

Read and trace each word.
Find and circle the matching word.

1. come

came   come   name

2. way

way   wag   pay

3. my

me   am   my

4. on

an   on   in

Write the word.

5. way   _____

6. on   _____

Bix the Dog

SUMMARY Bix the yellow Lab gets sick and visits the vet in this realistic story. Colorful photographs accompany the text.

LESSON VOCABULARY

she	take
up	what

INTRODUCE THE BOOK

INTRODUCE THE TITLE AND AUTHOR Discuss with children the title and the author of *Bix the Dog*. Ask: Who is Bix? What is happening to Bix?

BUILD BACKGROUND Discuss what happens when a pet animal gets sick. Ask: Do animals have special doctors? What are they called? Prompt children to recall what they know about veterinarians, based on personal experience, books, and television shows.

ELL Make sure that ELL children understand the role of a veterinarian. Provide a toy stethoscope, bandages, or other medical props and a stuffed animal and have children role-play a visit to the veterinarian.

PREVIEW Have children compare the book's cover and title page. Ask: Are any of the words the same? Is the picture the same? As children look through the book, help them generate questions about the photos. Think aloud: I wonder what is going to happen to the dog?

READ THE BOOK

SET PURPOSE Help children set a purpose for reading *Bix the Dog*. Think aloud: I wonder why the dog goes to the doctor. Let's read and find out.

STRATEGY SUPPORT: SUMMARIZE Having children recall a story and retell it in their own words helps them focus on important story events and decide whether the events could really happen or are make-believe.

COMPREHENSION QUESTIONS

PAGE 3 Why is Bix sad? *(Bix is sad because he is sick.)*

PAGE 4 Who is taking Bix to see the vet? *(Possible response: Bix's owner is taking him to the vet.)*

PAGE 5 What is the vet doing? How can she fix Bix up? Could this really happen? *(The vet is examining Bix with a stethoscope. She might give him medicine to make him feel better. This could really happen.)*

PAGE 6 Tell the story in your own words. Tell what happened first, next, and last. *(Responses will vary, but should include beginning, middle, and ending events.)*

REVISIT THE BOOK

THINK AND SHARE

1. First: Bix is in the van. Next: Bix goes to the vet. Last: Bix gets the paper.
2. Bix goes to the doctor; he gets examined; he feels better.
3. *Bix, fix*
4. Possible response: I would take my pet to the vet.

EXTEND UNDERSTANDING As children read the book, guide them to pay close attention to details in the photographs. Help them notice the seatbelt on page 4 and the newspaper on page 6.

RESPONSE OPTIONS

WRITING Suggest that children choose their favorite part of the story to illustrate. Have them write a sentence or two to label their illustration.

SCIENCE CONNECTION

Encourage children to find out more about pet care. Suggest that they visit the library to find out what a dog needs to stay healthy and happy.

Skill Work

TEACH/REVIEW VOCABULARY

Print each vocabulary word on an index card. Read the words aloud as a group. Then hold up the word cards, one at a time. Say a sentence containing the word, pausing to allow children to read the word and complete the sentence. For instance: Peanut butter (and) jelly sandwiches are my favorite.

TARGET SKILL AND STRATEGY

PLOT Point out to children that every story has a beginning, middle, and end. These events make up the story's plot. As children read *Bix the Dog*, have them look for the beginning, middle, and end of the story.

SUMMARIZE Remind children that when they read, they can use their own words to tell what happened in the story. As children read *Bix the Dog*, encourage them to think about how they would describe the story to a friend who hasn't read it.

ADDITIONAL SKILL INSTRUCTION

SEQUENCE OF EVENTS Point out to children that understanding what happens first, next, and last in a story helps them remember the story. Demonstrate a three-step process. (For instance, stand up, walk to the board, and write a word.) Ask children to describe what happened first, next, and last. After children have read *Bix the Dog*, ask them the first thing, the next thing, and the last thing that happened in the story.

Name _____

Plot

Read the sentences. Circle the word that shows where each sentence belongs in the story.

1. Bix is in the van.

   Beginning   Middle   End

2. Bix gets the paper.

   Beginning   Middle   End

3. Bix is at the vet.

   Beginning   Middle   End

Draw a picture of your favorite part of the story.

Bix the Dog

Name _____

Vocabulary

Read and trace each word.

1. take

2. she

3. what

4. up

Write each word.

_____

5. take   _____

_____

6. she   _____

_____

7. what   _____

_____

8. up   _____

On the Farm

SUMMARY A boy named Rob and his dog Socks help Rob's mom around the farm in this illustrated story.

LESSON VOCABULARY

blue	from
get	help
little	use

INTRODUCE THE BOOK

INTRODUCE THE TITLE AND AUTHOR Discuss with children the title and author of *On the Farm*. Ask: What does the illustrator do? Ask children to look at the cover illustration and predict where the story might take place.

BUILD BACKGROUND Draw a circle on the board and write the word *farm* in the center. Ask: Do you know what a farm is? Write children's ideas in the circle. Draw another circle and write the word *buildings* inside. Ask children to name buildings they might find on a farm. List these ideas in the *buildings* circle. Expand the farm concept map by drawing circles with additional labels, such as animals, buildings, or jobs. Connect each circle with a line to the "farm" circle.

PREVIEW/TAKE A PICTURE WALK Invite children to look through the book with you. Turn to page 3 and have them compare this illustration to the cover. Ask: Is this the same picture? As children preview the remaining pages, focus their attention on what the boy is doing in each picture. Model interesting vocabulary as you describe the boy's actions. For example, turn to page 4 and say: "The boy is feeding the hogs. What the hogs are eating is called *slop*. Slopping the hogs is another way of saying feeding the hogs." Continue with the rest of the illustrations.

READ THE BOOK

SET PURPOSE Guide children to set a purpose for reading *On the Farm*. Suggest that they compare the farm in the story to what they already know about farms. What things are the same? What things are different?

STRATEGY SUPPORT: VISUALIZE PREDICTIONS Tell children that picturing events can help them better remember the story. After reading page 3, have children close their eyes. Reread the page aloud to them and ask them to form a picture of it in their minds. Have them share with the class what they are seeing.

COMPREHENSION QUESTIONS

PAGE 3 Why do you think the dog is named Socks? *(The markings on the dog's legs look like socks.)*

PAGES 4–6 How did Socks get so muddy? Why does Rob wash the dog but not the hogs? *(Socks got muddy when Rob was feeding the hogs. Possible response: Rob washes Socks because Socks would get the car dirty.)*

PAGES 3–6 Name the jobs Rob does on the farm. Do you think a boy could really do these jobs? Why or why not? *(Rob helps to wipe the tractor, feed the hogs, wash the dog, and fix the wall. Responses will vary but should relate to children's experience.)*

PAGES 3–6 Does Rob like working on the farm? Why do you think so? *(Rob seems to like working on the farm; he is always smiling.)*

PAGE 7 What do you think Rob, Mom, and Socks will do when they get to town? *(Responses will vary.)*

REVISIT THE BOOK

THINK AND SHARE

1. Drawings may vary but should show a farm setting.
2. They might drive to the store to buy food.
3. *rags, pails, rocks*
4. Possible response: Rob and Socks could feed the other animals.

EXTEND UNDERSTANDING Ask children to consider whether the story could take place in a different setting. Ask: If Rob and Socks lived in a city, what jobs would they do? What would be the same? What would be different?

RESPONSE OPTIONS

WRITING Suggest that children retell the story from Rob's perspective. Ask them to imagine what Rob might think and say about his daily activities. Have children write and illustrate a few sentences, using pronouns as appropriate.

SOCIAL STUDIES CONNECTION

Encourage children to learn more about tractors and other farm equipment. Gather resources from the library, the Internet, or your local farm bureau. Children can make a class book that describes farm machines.

Skill Work

TEACH/REVIEW VOCABULARY

Write the word *help* on the board. Have children read it aloud and talk about what it means. Then turn to page 6. Read the text together, pausing before *help*. Ask a volunteer to highlight the word on the page with highlighting tape. Repeat for *use* (pages 3–6) and *blue* (page 6).

ELL Write each vocabulary word on a word card. Invite English language learners to go on a word hunt. Provide each child with a word card and a self-stick note and have children search the classroom for their chosen word. When they find the word, have them mark it with a self-stick note. Switch cards and play again.

TARGET SKILL AND STRATEGY

CHARACTER AND SETTING Point out to children that stories have people or animals in them (*characters*) and occur in a certain place or time (*setting*). Thinking about who is in a story and where it takes place helps readers understand what they read. Discuss Rob's attitudes and behaviors with the children. Ask: When Rob helps Mom with the hogs, what does this tell you about him? Would you like Rob to be your friend? Also discuss the setting of the story. Ask: Where does this story happen? Have you ever seen a place like this?

VISUALIZE Explain to children that good readers form pictures in their minds when they read a story. *Visualizing* helps readers understand what they are reading. Model as children read *On the Farm*: When I close my eyes, I can see a boy, his mom, and a dog on a farm. They are having a good time fixing it up. They are laughing while they feed the animals. The dog is getting very muddy.

ADDITIONAL SKILL INSTRUCTION

PLOT Point out to children that every story has three parts: beginning, middle, and end. Work with children to identify the beginning, middle, and end of *On the Farm*. Record these events on a simple story map.

Name_____

Character and Setting

Rob and Socks help Mom with the hogs.
Rob and Socks use rocks to fix the wall.
Rob and Socks go to town with Mom.

Draw two things that Rob does to help Mom.
Show where the story takes place. Show how Rob feels.

Name_____

Vocabulary

Circle the correct word to finish each sentence. Write the word on the line.

1. Rob and Mom have _____ soap.

   blue   black

2. Mom drives _____ the barn.

   farm   from

3. Rob and Socks _____ Mom on the farm.

   help   hall

4. Rob and Mom use _____ rags.

   like   little

5. Rob will _____ a hose to wash Socks.

   us   use

6. Mom will _____ the car.

   get   go

Time for Dinner

SUMMARY In this realistic story, a boy and his mother feed the animals in the barnyard before sitting down to share an evening meal. The story is written in predictable language, with strong illustration support.

LESSON VOCABULARY

eat	five
four	her
this	too

INTRODUCE THE BOOK

INTRODUCE THE TITLE AND AUTHOR Discuss with children the title and the author of *Time for Dinner.* Talk about the roles of the author and the illustrator. Look at the cover together and ask children to describe what the animals are doing in the illustration. Based on the title and the cover illustration, ask children what they think this story might be about. Who is eating dinner in the picture? Who else might eat dinner in the story?

BUILD BACKGROUND Sing "Old McDonald Had a Farm" with the children. Then involve the group in a discussion about farm life. Remind children of other stories they have read or heard about life on a farm. Talk about the kinds of animals that live on a farm and the role of the farmer in caring for them. Together, brainstorm a list of jobs to be done on a farm. Then ask children to think about how kids might help with this work. Ask: What kinds of jobs could a boy or girl your age do on a farm?

ELL Make sure that English language learners know the names of the farm animals pictured in this story. Use pictures of farm animals to play a matching game in which you call out the sound the animal makes and the children point to the picture and name the animal.

PREVIEW Invite children to look through the book and scan the illustrations. Encourage them to predict what might happen in this story, based on what they see. Point out the boy and his mother on page 3 and discuss the setting of the story and the characters' clothing. Ask children to identify the foods that the animals are eating on pages 4 and 5. Turn to page 7 and ask children to predict how the book might end. Introduce the word *picnic.* If children have experiences eating outdoors, encourage them to talk about this.

READ THE BOOK

SET PURPOSE Help children set a purpose for reading *Time for Dinner.* Ask children to review the predictions they made while previewing the illustrations. Suggest that children choose a prediction and look for the answer as they read. Model setting a purpose for reading: "It looks like the boy is helping his mother. I want to read and find out exactly what they are doing."

STRATEGY SUPPORT: IMPORTANT IDEAS Explain to children that a story can have many important ideas. While reading, have children determine whether an idea is important to the story. For example, model on page 3: Since the title of this book is *Time for Dinner,* I think the horses eating dinner is an important idea.

COMPREHENSION QUESTIONS

PAGE 3 What is this page mostly about? (*The page is about horses eating.*)

PAGE 4 What are these little animals? What are they eating? (*The little animals are chickens; they are eating grain.*)

PAGE 6 How do the boy and his mother know that it's time for dinner? (*They know it is time for dinner because the mother checked her watch.*)

PAGE 7 What did you know about what animals eat before you read this story? (*Responses will vary.*)

REVISIT THE BOOK

THINK AND SHARE

1. Possible response: The story is about dinner. People and animals all eat.
2. Possible response: I learned that different animals eat different things. Every page shows a different kind of food.
3. *eats, looking*
4. Possible response: Animals can rest at other times of the day.

EXTEND UNDERSTANDING Direct children's attention to the illustrations. Challenge them to find the animal that eats people's leftovers. Ask: What do you think the pig might eat for dinner the next day? Why do you think so?

RESPONSE OPTIONS

WRITING Invite children to write and illustrate a story about animals eating dinner in a different setting. They might write about animals in the forest, the jungle, or the zoo. Encourage them to use a predictable sentence pattern, as modeled in *Time for Dinner*.

DRAMA CONNECTION

Invite children to make stick puppets of the various farm animals featured in *Time for Dinner* and use them to dramatize the story. Together, make up dialogue for each of the characters in the story.

Skill Work

TEACH/REVIEW VOCABULARY

Write the word *eat* on the board. Read the word together and use it in a sentence. Turn to page 5 and ask children if they can find the word that contains *eat*. Read *eats* together. Repeat for the other vocabulary words.

TARGET SKILL AND STRATEGY

MAIN IDEA Turn to pages 4 and 5. Read the sentences together. Then ask: What are these sentences about? Help children understand that both pages are about eating dinner, and that this is the *main idea*. Repeat for other pages.

IMPORTANT IDEAS Explain to children that when they read, it helps to locate important ideas. Important ideas can tell more about the main idea of a story. Create a word web with *Dinner* in the center circle. Have children list important ideas from the story and add them to the outer circles of the web. (*horses eat hay, chicks eat grain, pigs eat scraps, people eat meals*)

ADDITIONAL SKILL INSTRUCTION

COMPARE AND CONTRAST Point out to children that they can think about how two things are *alike* and how they are *different*. Turn to pages 3 and 4. Read the text and model how to compare the horses to the chickens, using a Venn diagram. Compare characteristics such as where the animals live, how many feet they have, and what they eat. Repeat with pages 5, 6, and 7, asking children to compare the pig and the people.

Name _____

Main Idea

Read the sentences.

The cat eats this dinner.

The pig is eating her dinner.

The little dog is eating dinner.

Mom and I eat dinner too.

1. What are these sentences all about?

   a) the pig

   b) animals on the farm

   c) eating dinner

2. Draw a picture that shows the main idea.

Name _____

Vocabulary

Read and write each word. Find and circle the matching word.

Words to Know

eat	five	four	her	this	too

1. eat _____ cat, eat, fat

2. five _____ fine, five, fit

3. four _____ four, for, fire

4. her _____ her, hem, hen

5. this _____ that, thin, this

6. too _____ to, too, boo

At Your Vet

SUMMARY This fiction reader describes children taking animals to the vet. We also learn that the vet can help our pets.

LESSON VOCABULARY

saw	small
tree	your

INTRODUCE THE BOOK

INTRODUCE THE TITLE AND AUTHOR Discuss with children the title and the author of *At Your Vet.* Encourage children to share what they think this book will be about, based on the title. Ask: What animals do you think the vet helps?

BUILD BACKGROUND Invite children to share what they know about animals. Have them describe animals they have seen, at home or elsewhere. Encourage children to share what they know about these animals, including what they look like, what sounds they make, and how to care for them.

PREVIEW Have children preview the book by flipping through the pages and looking at the illustrations. Encourage children to describe what they see happening on each page. Ask: What animal(s) do you see here? What is this person doing with the animal(s)? Where are they?

READ THE BOOK

SET PURPOSE Based on your preview of the book, guide children in setting a purpose for reading. Ask them what they would like to learn or find out about the story. After looking at the illustrations, have children predict what animals they think they will learn about in the story. Encourage children to share their favorite illustrations and why they would like to know more about these animals, people, or what they are doing.

STRATEGY SUPPORT: STORY STRUCTURE Explain to children that stories are arranged in an order from beginning to end. Each event in the story leads to the next event. When they think about how all these events fit together, they can tell what the story is all about.

COMPREHENSION QUESTIONS

PAGE 3 What happened first in the story? (*He saw a sick bird.*)

PAGE 4 Then what did the boy do next? (*He took the bird to the vet.*)

PAGES 5–6 What other animal did the boy take to the vet? (*A small cat*)

PAGE 7 What did we learn from this story? (*Vets can help animals.*)

REVISIT THE BOOK

THINK AND SHARE

1. The story is mostly about small animals that visit the vet.
2. Possible response: Beginning: A boy sees and takes a bird to the vet. Middle: A boy sees and takes a cat to the vet. End: The vet helps the animals.
3. *grass*
4. Responses will vary but might include a parent, another relative, or a teacher.

EXTEND UNDERSTANDING Call children's attention to the *Animal Shelter* sign in the illustrations on pages 4 and 6. Help children read these words and discuss how this sign helps us better understand the story. Ask: Would it be as easy to understand where the characters were taking the animals if the *Animal Shelter* sign were not there? Encourage children to tell about the different signs and environmental print they see around them every day and how this information helps us.

RESPONSE OPTIONS

SPEAKING Write the following sentences on the board. *I saw a _____. Take the _____ to the vet.* Have children think of ways to complete the idea based on the story and then take turns saying the first sentence aloud to the class. The rest of the group then repeats the second sentence to complete the exchange. You may wish to model how to do this to get children started. Say: I saw a sick hamster. Then have the children say: Take the hamster to the vet.

SCIENCE CONNECTION

Explore different ways we can help animals. Discuss with children why we take animals to the vet and what shelters or other rescue organizations can do for animals. If possible, invite a veterinarian or animal rescue worker to come speak to the class.

Skill Work

TEACH/REVIEW VOCABULARY

Have children write down each of the vocabulary words on their own papers saying the words as they do so. Help children think of sentences using each word and repeat these to each other.

ELL Encourage English language learners to say the vocabulary words in their home languages and write the words on their papers. Give them sentences using each word and ask them to repeat the sentences.

TARGET SKILL AND STRATEGY

MAIN IDEA Tell children that a *main idea* is what a story is all about. Guide children in identifying the main idea of *At Your Vet* by asking: What is happening on pages 4 and 6 of this story? Children should tell you that the boy is taking a sick animal to the vet.

STORY STRUCTURE Remind children that each event in a story leads to the next. Together, these events show what the story is all about. Ask: What happens in the beginning? What happens next? What happens at the end?

ADDITIONAL SKILL INSTRUCTION

THEME Explain to the children that every story has a "big idea" or theme. This "big idea" is what the story is all about, and might even be a lesson that we learn from the story. Guide children in determining the big idea in *At Your Vet*. Model for them how to determine the big idea. Ask: What did we learn from reading this book? What is this story all about?

Name _____

Main Idea

Think about what you read in *At Your Vet*.
Circle the answer to the question.

1. What is the book about?

   a. going to the doctor

   b. helping animals

   c. feeding birds

Read the sentences below.

> I like to take care of my dog. I walk her every
> day. I feed her every day. We play with toys. She
> sleeps in my bed.

2. What are the sentences mostly about? Circle the answer.

   a. cleaning a room   **c.** taking care of a dog

   b. playing with toys   **d.** taking a walk

3. Draw a picture of you or a friend taking care of a pet.

Name _____

Vocabulary

Write the word from the box that best completes each sentence.

Words to Know
saw   small   tree   your

1. The cat was _____ .

2. I _____ a dog.

3. The vet can help _____ pets.

4. The bird was in the _____ .

5. The word *saw* has more than one meaning. Draw a picture that shows another meaning of *saw*.

Fun in the Sun

SUMMARY Children learn how animals cool down in the hot sun. Photographs of animals playing in the water capture children's imagination and activate their experiences of playing in water.

LESSON VOCABULARY

home	into
many	them

INTRODUCE THE BOOK

INTRODUCE THE TITLE AND AUTHOR Discuss the title and the author of *Fun in the Sun*. Ask children to look at the photograph on the cover and comment on how it relates to the title. Ask children in what kind of area the book might take place.

BUILD BACKGROUND Encourage discussion about what children do on a hot summer day. Ask: Do you like to drink cold lemonade? Do you like to play with a hose or swim? How does water make you feel?

PREVIEW Have children look at each picture in the book. Encourage them to name the animals they can. Ask if any children have seen any of the animals in other contexts, such as at a zoo or in another book.

READ THE BOOK

SET PURPOSE Model how to set a purpose for reading by commenting on the photograph on the cover. Say: "The sun looks very hot! I want to read this book to see what animals do when it is very hot." Prompt students to tell their own purposes for reading the book.

STRATEGY SUPPORT: TEXT STRUCTURE As children read the story, call their attention to how the text is organized. Explain that sometimes an author will repeat words or phrases so that readers will better remember the information. Ask: Which words do you see repeated a lot in this story? *(many, animals, hot, pond)*

COMPREHENSION QUESTIONS

PAGE 4 Why is it hot? *(because the sun is shining)*

PAGE 5 What are the hippos doing in the photograph? *(They are cooling off in the pond.)*

PAGE 6 Where are the elephants going? *(They are going to the pond.)*

PAGE 7 Is the pond very deep? How do you know? *(no, because it only comes up to the tops of the zebras' legs)*

PAGE 8 Which animals use the pond to cool off? *(hippos, elephants, and zebras)*

REVISIT THE BOOK

THINK AND SHARE

1. Possible response: They went into a pond to cool off.
2. Possible response: I learned the same thing about each of them.
3. *fun, sun*
4. Page 8 shows three different kinds of animals.

EXTEND UNDERSTANDING Have children look at the photograph of the hippos on page 5. Ask: What can you learn about hippos from this photograph? *(Possible responses: They can open their mouths wide; they have tiny ears.)* Continue in a similar fashion with the other photographs.

RESPONSE OPTIONS

SPEAKING Have children describe to others what they do to stay cool.

ELL Write the words *elephant*, *hippo*, and *zebra* on a piece of paper, allowing room between each word. Make copies of the paper for each English language leaner and ask them to draw a picture of the animal underneath its name.

SCIENCE CONNECTION

Assist children in doing research on the African savannah and animals mentioned in *Fun in the Sun,* using books, children's wildlife magazines, and the Internet. Have each child choose one aspect of this environment and write a sentence about it. Then have children use large construction paper to make cutouts representing the characteristics or animals they have chosen. Attach their sentences to the backs of their cutouts. Create a savannah tableau with children standing, holding their cutouts, reading their sentences in turn. Invite another class to observe. Allow the children to answer questions about the parts of the savannah they represent.

Skill Work

TEACH/REVIEW VOCABULARY

Have children take turns using each vocabulary word in a sentence. Have them say their sentences aloud to the group as you write their sentences on the board.

ELL Many children, especially English language learners, think of *home* and *house* as completely interchangeable. Explain the meaning of *house* as the building in which people or certain animals live, while the broader meaning of *home* includes houses, places, countries, and habitats.

TARGET SKILL AND STRATEGY

CAUSE AND EFFECT Draw attention to *cause-and-effect* relationships by asking children to think as they read about what is happening and why those things are happening. Say: Look at pages 5, 6, and 7. What happened? Why did it happen?

TEXT STRUCTURE Remind children that paying attention to text structure will help them better remember what they have read. It will also help them predict what might come next in the text. Say: Rhinos are another type of animal that like hot weather. What do you think the author would say about rhinos in this story? *(Many hot rhinos go into a pond.)*.

ADDITIONAL SKILL INSTRUCTION

AUTHOR'S PURPOSE Begin prompting children to identify the *author's purpose* by identifying the author. Before children read the book, ask: Who wrote this book? What do you think the book will be about? Why? How do you think you will feel or think about animals and the sun after reading this book? Why? Do you think this book is funny, sad, serious, or exciting? Lead children to explain their answers by identifying features or facts in the text. Record children's answers to discuss after reading. Allow for multiple correct responses to emphasize that authors can have more than one purpose.

Name _____

Cause and Effect

Think about what happened in the story. Then think about why it happened. Write a word from the story that best fits into each sentence.

1. The sun is _____ .

2. Animals have _____ in the sun.

3. The animals are hot. So they run into a _____ .

4. Draw a picture of something you like to do when you are hot.

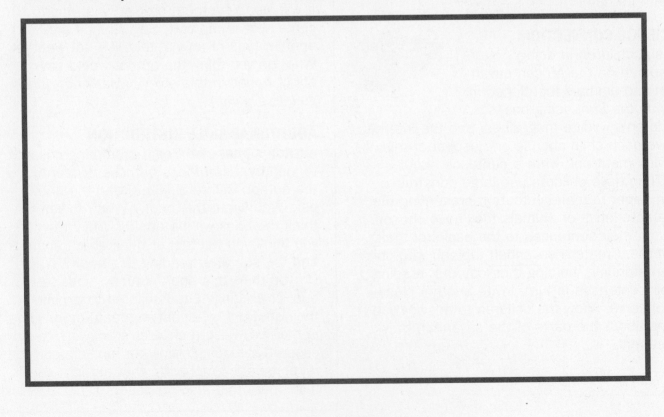

Name _____

Vocabulary

Draw a picture of the meaning of the word in each box.

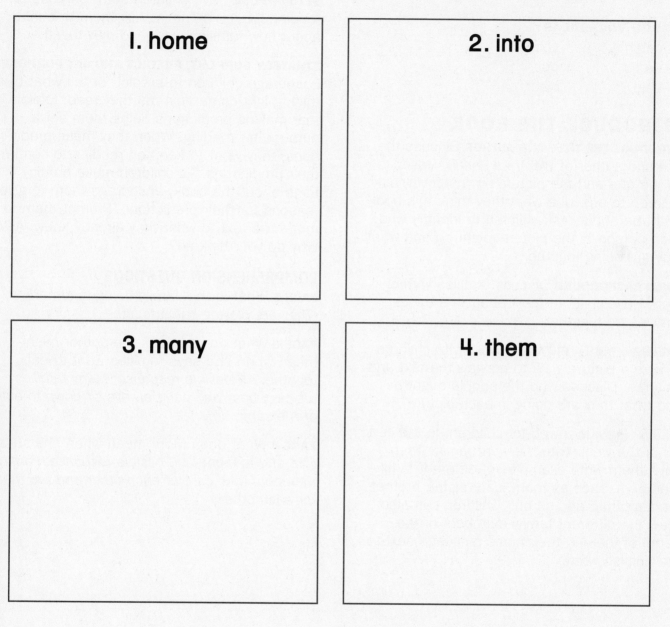

1. home	2. into
3. many	4. them

We Are a Family

SUMMARY Children read about families and the things they do together.

LESSON VOCABULARY

catch	good
no	put
said	want

INTRODUCE THE BOOK

INTRODUCE THE TITLE AND AUTHOR Discuss the title and author of *We Are a Family*. Based on the title and the picture on the cover, ask children to describe what they think this book might be about. Ask children to identify who each person in the picture might be and what they are doing together.

BUILD BACKGROUND Discuss families with children. Have children think about the things families do together.

PREVIEW/TAKE A PICTURE WALK Invite children to take a picture walk to preview the text and pictures. Discuss who the people might be and what they are doing in each picture.

ELL Provide a web for children. In the center of the web, write the word *family*. Then have them write examples of different family members, such as mom, dad, sister, brother, grandmother, and so on. Children can also draw the different family members or the name of them in their home language next to the English word.

READ THE BOOK

SET PURPOSE Have children set a purpose for reading *We Are a Family*. Ask them to think about how families work and play together.

STRATEGY SUPPORT: PREDICT AND SET PURPOSE Encourage children to predict, or tell what they think might come next, as they read. Explain that making predictions helps them set a purpose for reading. When they make predictions, they want to keep on reading to confirm their predictions. As children make predictions about the book, encourage them to give reasons for their predictions. Prompt them to relate the text to what they already know. Ask: Why do you think so?

COMPREHENSION QUESTIONS

PAGE 5 What is this family doing together? *(They are playing catch together.)*

PAGE 6 What do you think the author might mean when she says families *want* to eat together? *(Possible response: Many families are very busy and can't always sit down to eat at the same time.)*

PAGE 8 What does Mom mean when she says, "No one is alone"? *(Possible response: Family members take care of each other and are there for each other.)*

REVISIT THE BOOK

THINK AND SHARE

1. Possible responses: went shopping,; put things away; played catch; ate; read.
2. Possible response: The family might go to sleep, because the last picture shows them in bed in their pajamas.
3. The word *want* is on page 6. Possible responses: The word *want* means to desire or wish for. I *want* a puppy.
4. Possible responses: My family goes shopping, plays games, and walks together. I would like to go camping with my family.

EXTEND UNDERSTANDING Explain to children that all families are different. For example, some families have many children, while others have only one child. Some families have only a mother or father, some have both, while others also include grandparents or aunts and uncles. Ask children to describe their own families.

RESPONSE OPTIONS

WRITING Begin a class chart with the predictable sentence pattern *We _____ together.* Complete the first sentence and then ask each child to suggest a way to complete the sentence by filling in the blank with something he or she does with his or her family. Write the children's sentences on the chart. Read the chart together. Invite children to copy and illustrate their sentences to make a class book.

DRAMA CONNECTION

Divide children into groups of three to five. Have each group think of an activity that families do together and come up with a way to mime that activity. Have each group perform their mime for the rest of the class. After each group performs, the rest of the class can try to guess the activity the group acted out. Have children act out as many activities as you have time for.

Skill Work

TEACH/REVIEW VOCABULARY

Print the vocabulary words on index cards. Display each card and read the word aloud as a group. Hand a card to different children. Then write the beginning letter of one of the words on the board and ask the child who has the word that begins with that letter to come to the board and complete the word. Read the word aloud as a group. Continue until all words have been written. If there's time, pass the cards to different children and repeat the activity.

TARGET SKILL AND STRATEGY

SEQUENCE Remind children that in a story, something happens first, something happens next, and something happens last. After reading *We Are a Family*, have a group of three to four children recall and then act out what the families in the book did first, next, and last.

PREDICT AND SET PURPOSE Remind children that when they make a prediction, they think about what might happen next in a story. Point out that after they make a prediction they should confirm their prediction by reading the part that tells them what happened next.

ADDITIONAL SKILL INSTRUCTION

DRAW CONCLUSIONS Remind children that as they read, they can use what they have already read and what they already know about their own lives to figure out more about the information and events in a book. Model drawing conclusions. Say: At the end of *We Are a Family*, I can guess that the family is probably getting ready to go to bed. I think this because everyone in the picture is in his or her pajamas and they are playing on a bed. At my house, we all sleep in our favorite pajamas!

Name _____

Sequence

Think about *We Are a Family*. Write 1, 2, and 3 to tell what happened first, next, and last. Draw a picture to show each one.

1. The family eats together.

_____

- -

_____

2. The family shops together.

_____

- -

_____

3. The family reads together.

_____

- -

_____

1.	2.	3.

Name _____

Vocabulary

Read and trace each word.
Find and circle the matching word.

1. put

pat   pot   put

2. good

gold   good   goof

3. said

sad   side   said

4. want

want   what   watt

Write the word.

5. no _____

6. catch _____

The Class Play

SUMMARY In *The Class Play*, a class works together to stage a dramatic performance for their parents. The simple, repetitive text describes each step of the preparation process.

LESSON VOCABULARY

be	could	horse
of	old	paper

INTRODUCE THE BOOK

INTRODUCE THE TITLE AND AUTHOR Discuss with children the title and author of *The Class Play*. Ask children what kinds of things they might expect to read about in a book called *The Class Play*. Examine the cover illustration together and encourage children to describe the various costumes the characters in the book are wearing. Turn to the title page and compare the illustration on this page to the cover illustration. Ask children to read the title and names of the author and illustrator. Point out that the title page always contains this information.

BUILD BACKGROUND Invite children to discuss their personal experience with plays. If children have performed in a play, ask them to talk about what they did to prepare for the show. If children have attended a play, discuss the roles of the performers and the audience.

PREVIEW Lead children on a picture walk through the book. Turn to page 3. Point out the teacher and the children in the class. On page 4, invite children to guess what the teacher might be saying. On page 6, ask children to describe what the boy is doing. Together, describe what is happening in the final scene. Ask children if they think this is the beginning of the play or the end, and why.

READ THE BOOK

SET PURPOSE Support children as they set a purpose for reading *The Class Play*. Suggest that children choose a character from the cover illustration to learn more about. Let them know that after they finish reading *The Class Play*, they will talk about what has happened in the story and why it happened.

STRATEGY SUPPORT: MONITOR AND CLARIFY Remind children to think aloud and to use pictures to help them understand the words as they read. Model the process. For instance: "I don't understand how Nate can make a tree. Let's look at the illustration and see." Suggest that children read in pairs, thinking aloud and pointing out details in the illustrations to one another.

COMPREHENSION QUESTIONS

PAGE 3 Why do you think the children are raising their hands in this picture? (*Possible response: The children are raising their hands because they have something to say.*)

PAGE 4 What do you think the teacher is reading to Kate? (*Possible response: She is reading a script.*)

PAGE 6 Why is Nate making trees for the stage? (*Possible response: He is making trees for the stage because the class needs props for its play.*)

PAGE 7 What was this story mostly about? What might be a good title for the children's play? (*The story was about putting on a play. Responses will vary, but should draw on information from the book.*)

REVISIT THE BOOK

THINK AND SHARE

1. Possible response: They are putting on a play.
2. They make a horse mask.
3. Kate, Jake, Grace, Nate
4. Possible responses: The play is funny. They are proud of their children.

EXTEND UNDERSTANDING Discuss with children how the illustrations enhance the meaning of the story. Ask them to think about how the pictures match the words and think about other ways the book could have been illustrated.

RESPONSE OPTIONS

WRITING Have children write and illustrate an alternate ending to the story, imitating the sentence pattern. For instance: What could the parents do? They will smile and clap. Encourage children to read their pages to their classmates.

DRAMA CONNECTIONS Help children plan a performance of a favorite story to share with their classmates. Together, plan who will perform each role, who will help make the costumes, and who will assemble the props.

Skill Work

TEACH/REVIEW VOCABULARY

Write the vocabulary words on the board. Read the words together. Ask children to locate each word in the text and mark it with highlighting tape. Print the words on index cards and let children take turns selecting a card and saying it in a sentence.

ELL Invite English language learners to play a guessing game with vocabulary cards. Stack word cards facedown. Have children take turns selecting a card and making up a riddle about the spelling or meaning of the word for the group to guess.

TARGET SKILL AND STRATEGY

CAUSE AND EFFECT Point out to children that when they read a story, they can think about what happened (effect) and why it happened (cause). Provide an example: Drop a book on the floor and have children listen for the loud noise. Discuss how the noise occurred because the book was dropped. As children read The Class Play, ask specific questions to guide their thinking about what happens and why. Ask: Why did Grace and Jake make a horse? Why did the grownups come to the auditorium?

MONITOR AND CLARIFY Remind children that what they read should make sense. Good readers ask themselves questions to make sure that they understand what they are reading. If they are confused about what is happening and why it is happening, they should look at the illustrations to help them understand.

ADDITIONAL SKILL INSTRUCTION

MAIN IDEA Display an illustration from a book the group has recently read and ask children to tell what the picture is all about. Point out that stories, just like pictures, are about something and that children can use their own words to tell what a story is about. After children have read The Class Play, turn back to selected pages and ask: What are these sentences mostly about? How can you tell?

Name_____

Cause and Effect

Read the sentences.
Circle the sentence that tells what happened.
Underline the sentence that tells why it happened.

1. Grace and Jake need a job to do. Grace and Jake will make a horse from old paper.

2. We need trees for the stage. Nate will make trees for the stage.

3. The play was funny. The parents smiled and laughed.

4. **Draw what happened.**   **Draw why it happened.**

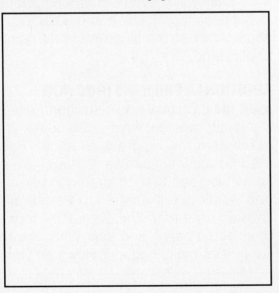   

Name_____

Vocabulary

Read the words in the box. Write each word on the line.

Words to Know
be   could   horse   of   old   paper

1. horse _____

2. old _____

3. be _____

4. paper _____

5. could _____

6. of _____

Here in My Neighborhood

SUMMARY In this story, a girl takes us on a tour of her neighborhood. We see people who live and work there, different shops, and a park to play in. We also get on and off a bus and meet a police officer. At the end we realize that a neighborhood can be a busy place.

LESSON VOCABULARY

live	out
people	who
work	

INTRODUCE THE BOOK

INTRODUCE THE TITLE AND AUTHOR Cover up the book title, and encourage children to explore and describe the cover illustration. Have them conclude where this scene takes place. Confirm that it is a neighborhood. Reveal the title and ask children if they see the word *neighborhood.* Help them read the book title, as well as the author's and illustrator's names.

BUILD BACKGROUND Invite children to describe their own neighborhoods, or the school neighborhood. Elicit from children specific details about the people, buildings, and other physical features they see in the neighborhood. Summarize that a neighborhood is a place where people live, work, shop, and play.

PREVIEW/TAKE A PICTURE WALK Let children look through the art in the book. On each page, have children find the person who might be telling the story. Call attention to the buildings in the background of page 5, and ask children what type of neighborhood this might be. *(a city)*

ELL Use plastic toy figures to help children learn the vocabulary words. Gather a group of figures, and say, "*People.*" Place the people inside a toy house, and say, "People *live* here." Use the figures to demonstrate and practice all words.

READ THE BOOK

SET PURPOSE Remind children that an author has a purpose, or a reason, for writing a book. Explain that readers can have a purpose for wanting to read a book, too, and encourage children to set a purpose for reading this book. For example, perhaps children are interested to know what the girl does for fun in her neighborhood. Tell children to look for the answers to their questions as they read.

STRATEGY SUPPORT: IMPORTANT IDEAS Remind children that authors can have many important ideas in a story. Understanding which ideas are important will help readers better understand the story. Suggest that children pause after each page to see if they can find an important idea. Say: Look at the question on page 4. What important idea is answered here? *(Pals live here and play ball.)*

COMPREHENSION QUESTIONS

PAGE 3 Why does the author start the book with people? *(Because the people are interesting; because the people have fun jobs)*

PAGE 4 What question might you ask to help you understand this page? *(What game are they playing? What game uses balls and bats?)*

PAGE 5 Who might Mitch be? How do you know? *(A friend; usually you call friends by their first names.)*

PAGE 7 What can you tell about Ms. Whit's job? *(She is probably a police officer because she is wearing a uniform.)*

REVIST THE BOOK

THINK AND SHARE

1. Possible responses: The author wants to show that people make the neighborhood special.

2. Possible responses: Many people live here. There is a lot to do in this neighborhood.

3. Possible responses:
1. Mitch bakes bread.
2. Chuck drives a bus.
3. Ms. Whit watches out for kids.

4. Possible responses: The neighborhood has some tall buildings. Different types of people live in this neighborhood.

EXTEND UNDERSTANDING Ask children to explain how this story ends, and agree that it ends with the girl and her father riding the bus. Encourage children to suggest places for where the girl and her father might be going. Prompt children to consider places in their neighborhood that might be in the girl's neighborhood too, such as a library, a mall, her grandparents' home, and so on.

RESPONSE OPTIONS

WRITING Have children copy the sentences, *This is my neighborhood. It is ___ .* Encourage children to complete the sentence starter with information about their neighborhoods. If time allows, let children draw pictures to illustrate their sentences.

WORD WORK Write the word *neighborhood* in the center of a word web. Then elicit from children words they associate with *neighborhood*, and write their words in the surrounding circles of the web. Encourage children to explain their word choices.

SOCIAL STUDIES CONNECTION

Invite children to compare their neighborhoods with the neighborhood they read about in the book. You might set up a Venn diagram to help children record and compare ideas.

Skill Work

TEACH/REVIEW VOCABULARY

Write the word *people* on the board, and help children read it. You might point out that in this word, the letters *eo* make the long e sound. Have children use the word *people* with the other vocabulary words. For example: *People live in neighborhoods. People work in neighborhoods. Who are the people in our neighborhood?*

TARGET SKILL AND STRATEGY

AUTHOR'S PURPOSE Mention to children that the *author's purpose* is the reason why an author chose to write a story. Speculate why an author might choose to write about a neighborhood. For example, the author may want to show people what it is like where he or she lives. Tell children that as they read, they should try to figure out the author's purpose.

IMPORTANT IDEAS Share with children that when they read, it helps to find important ideas in a story. Authors can organize a story so that important ideas are easier to find. Ask children how this story is organized. *(by questions and answers)* Explain that the answers the author gives are some of the important ideas of this story.

ADDITIONAL SKILL INSTRUCTION

DRAW CONCLUSIONS Explain that when they finish reading a story, they should try to put together what the book was trying to tell them. As they do so, they should consider their own knowledge about neighborhoods. Help children draw conclusions about this story. First, invite children to recall the details of this neighborhood. Next, have children express their own ideas about neighborhoods. Finally, have them combine all their ideas into a statement.

Name _____

Author's Purpose

Look at the picture and read the words.

I play in this park.
I see lots of people.
This is a busy place.

Why do you think the author wrote *Here in My Neighborhood*?
Use the words in the box to fill in the blanks.

| show | share | people | park |

1. The author likes the _____ .

2. The author wants to _____ a busy neighborhood.

3. The author cares about _____ in the neighborhood.

4. The author wants others to _____ her neighborhood.

Name _____

Vocabulary

Complete each sentence with a word from the box.
The pictures will help you to fill in the blanks.

Words to Know
live   out   people   who   work

1. This picture shows _____ .

2. People _____ in a _____ .

3. People _____ in a _____ .

4. _____ do you see here?

5. I like going _____ in my neighborhood!

Look at Dinosaurs

SUMMARY A dinosaur expert looks at dinosaur bones to help decide what the dinosaurs ate.

LESSON VOCABULARY

down	inside
now	there
together	

INTRODUCE THE BOOK

INTRODUCE THE TITLE AND AUTHOR Discuss with children the title and author of *Look at Dinosaurs*. Ask: Looking at the cover, where do you think the dinosaurs are? Is this a picture of a time like today or long ago? Turn to the title page. Ask: Where do you think this woman is?

BUILD BACKGROUND Have children share their knowledge of dinosaurs and any experiences of seeing fossils and dinosaur exhibits. Ask them if they think dinosaurs ate meat, plants, or both.

PREVIEW/TAKE A PICTURE WALK Invite children to look at the pictures in the book before reading. Discuss what children think is happening in the pictures. Point out that there is a thought bubble on page 4 that shows the woman is thinking about dinosaurs. Ask children to tell you what they think is going to happen to the bones on page 5. Ask them to tell the differences they see between the dinosaurs on pages 6 and 7.

READ THE BOOK

SET PURPOSE Have children set a purpose for reading *Look at Dinosaurs*. Children's interest in dinosaurs should guide this purpose. Suggest that children think about what different dinosaurs might eat and how people can find out about dinosaurs.

STRATEGY SUPPORT: INFERRING Tell children that *inferring* means to take information from the text and combine it with what you already know to learn something new. Model using pages 7–8 to make an inference about what types of dinosaurs existed. Say: I see that one type of dinosaur is eating plants and another is eating meat. I know that dinosaurs had special features that helped them get food more easily. I can infer that the dinosaur on page 7 has a long neck so it can get plants up high. The dinosaur on page 8 has sharp teeth and claws so it can eat meat.

COMPREHENSION QUESTIONS

PAGE 3 The people in this picture have just found some dinosaur bones. What do you think they will do with them? *(Possible response: put them in a museum)*

PAGE 5 What is the woman's job? *(Possible response: to look at dinosaur bones and figure out what dinosaurs ate)*

PAGE 6 What is the big dinosaur on the page doing? *(Possible response: It is about to eat a tree.)*

PAGE 7 What do you think the dinosaur on this page is going to eat? *(Possible response: the little green lizard)*

PAGE 8 What on this page can help you understand what the words say? *(The picture can help.)*

REVISIT THE BOOK

THINK AND SHARE

1. First: plants; Next: meat
2. We look at the bones.
3. *We'll*
4. The reader should first point to the dinosaur on page 6 and then the one on page 7.

EXTEND UNDERSTANDING Ask children how having people in the same picture as the finished dinosaur model helped them to understand how big some dinosaurs were. (See page 8.) Then ask children which were their favorite pictures and have them explain why.

RESPONSE OPTIONS

VIEWING Make other picture books about dinosaurs available to the class. Invite children to look through the books and see many different kinds of dinosaurs. Have children write their names on small, self-stick note papers. Have children stick their names on different pictures of dinosaurs (one name per page). Call on each child to show his or her picture and tell whether the dinosaur would eat meat or plants and why.

SCIENCE CONNECTION

Display a variety of picture books about dinosaurs. Invite children to look through the books to see what different dinosaurs looked like and where they might have lived. Afterwards encourage children to describe the different dinosaurs.

Skill Work

TEACH/REVIEW VOCABULARY

Make vocabulary word cards. Have children pick a word when you call out that word's opposite. (*Up/down, outside/inside, here/there, alone/together*)

ELL To make sure children understand information in the text, have them point to pictures that illustrate the following words: *dinosaur* and *bones*. For the word *meat*, use pictures in classroom books to show different examples of meat.

TARGET SKILL AND STRATEGY

SEQUENCE Tell children that a good way to understand information in a book is to think about what happens first, next, and last. To help students better understand the information in *Look at Dinosaurs*, write the following on sentence strips: *Seeing what the dinosaur looked like. Putting the bones together. Finding bones.* Then help children put the sentences in a sequence that makes the most sense. (*Finding bones, putting bones together, seeing what the dinosaur looked like.*)

INFERRING Remind children that as they read, they should think about the information in the text and pictures along with what they already know. They can use this information to find out something new. Have children infer what must have taken place from the pictures on page 3, 5, and 8. (*Possible response: Scientists found the bones of a dinosaur. A scientist put the bones together. People can now see the dinosaur at a museum.*)

ADDITIONAL SKILL INSTRUCTION

CAUSE AND EFFECT Tell children that as they read they should think about what happened and why it happened. In *Look at Dinosaurs*, people are looking at dinosaur bones. Note that the bones are displayed in a museum. Ask why the bones might be in the museum. Tell children that the bones being shown in the museum is what happened and why it happened is because people want to learn more about dinosaurs.

Name _____

Sequence

Think about *Look at Dinosaurs*. Write 1, 2, and 3 to tell what happened first, next, and last. Draw a picture to show each step.

_____ Dinosaurs died.

_____ Dinosaurs lived.

_____ We study dinosaurs' bones.

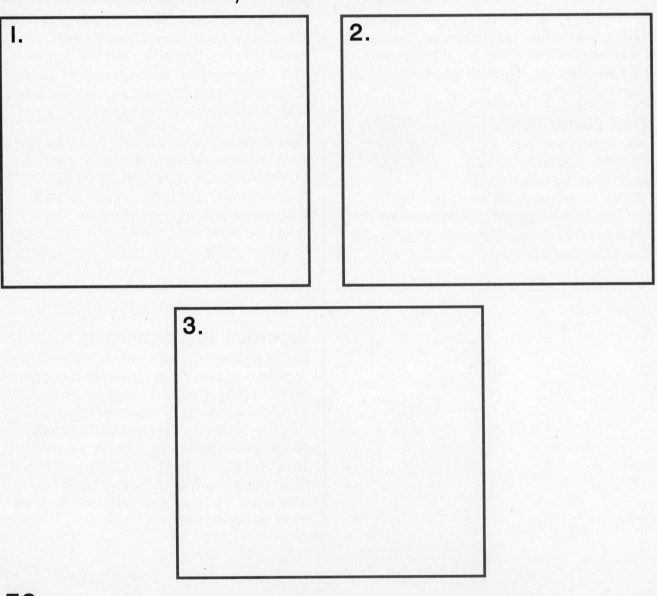

1.

2.

3.

Name _____

Vocabulary

Circle the picture that shows the word.

1. down

2. together

3. inside

Next to each word, write a sentence using that word.

4. there

5. now

Around the Forest

SUMMARY Many plants and animals live in forests. In the fall, some leaves turn yellow and red. In this text, readers see the forest through the eyes of two children.

LESSON VOCABULARY

around	find	food
grow	under	water

INTRODUCE THE BOOK

INTRODUCE THE TITLE AND AUTHOR Read the title and the author's name, and invite children to read them with you. Write the word *forest* on the board, and say it several times with the group so they become familiar with it. Then discuss the images on the book cover, and ask children what shapes they see. Confirm for children that these shapes are trees. Speculate with children how the shapes might relate to the content of the book.

BUILD BACKGROUND Share with children that forests are places where plants and animals live. Invite children to predict what plants and animals they might see if they visited a forest. Ask: Do you think you will see in this book some of the plants and animals you have named?

PREVIEW Invite children to take a picture walk through this book. Encourage children to point out the first thing they notice. Many children might call attention to the shapes in which the photographs have been placed. Challenge children to identify the shapes they see.

READ THE BOOK

SET PURPOSE Help children set a purpose for reading, based on their own interest in plants, animals, or other things related to the topic. Encourage children to select a photo they might like to know more about.

STRATEGY SUPPORT: BACKGROUND KNOWLEDGE Remind children that using what they already know can help them better understand what they read. Before reading, have children discuss what they already know about where types of animals live in a forest.

COMPREHENSION QUESTIONS

PAGE 3 Why does the author include two children in this book? (*Possible response: The author wants readers to see the forest as it is experienced by two children. The author hopes other children will want to visit a forest, like the children in the book.*)

PAGE 5 In which season do leaves turn yellow? (*in the fall*)

PAGE 6 Look at this picture. What do you think we might read about on this page? (*Possible response: squirrel, nut, animals, forest*)

PAGE 8 If you watched birds in a forest, what might you see them do? (*Possible response: fly, sit on a branch, sing, look for food*)

REVISIT THE BOOK

THINK AND SHARE

1. Possible response: The author wanted to show readers that the forest is a fun and interesting place.

2. Possible response: I knew bears lived in forests. It helped me see that lots of animals live in the forest.

3. *looked*

4. Possible response: Responses will vary but should include mention of trees or pictured aspects of the forest.

EXTEND UNDERSTANDING Work with children to make the connection between the shape on each page and the photograph within. For example, the shape on page 5 is a leaf; the photograph shows yellow leaves in the fall. Let children have fun suggesting other shapes and photographs that could be included in a book about forests.

RESPONSE OPTIONS

WORD WORK Say *forest*, and invite children to share words they think of when they hear this word. List words on the board. Circle words that appear in the book. Organize the words into groups, such as animal words, plant words, weather words, and descriptive words. Conclude by asking children to draw and cut out leaf shapes. Have children write one word inside each leaf shape. Then arrange the leaf shapes on the branches of a bulletin board tree titled, "A Forest of Words."

SCIENCE CONNECTION

Set up a Venn diagram, and label one side *Mammals* and one side *Birds.* Tell children that squirrels and bears are mammals, and ask children to list their physical features. Examples could include fur, four legs, can't fly, and live babies. Then ask children how birds differ from mammals, and elicit ideas for the Venn diagram, such as feathers, wings, two legs, can fly, and babies hatch from eggs.

Skill Work

TEACH/REVIEW VOCABULARY

Write sentences on the board for each vocabulary word. Say the word, then ask children to read the sentence and find the word in the sentence. Talk about the meaning of the word in the context of the sentence.

ELL Bring a plant to class, invite a child to water the plant, and say *water*. Using the plant as a reference, use gestures to help children understand the meaning of *around*, *find, food, grow,* and *under*. Have children repeat each word, imitating gestures.

TARGET SKILL AND STRATEGY

AUTHOR'S PURPOSE Explain that an *author's purpose* is the reason why an author chose to write something. Speculate with children why the author might have chosen to write this book. Let children exchange ideas; for example, this author may want readers to learn about a forest.

BACKGROUND KNOWLEDGE Mention to children that they can use what they already know to help understand what they read. Lead children in a discussion about experiences they have had visiting forests or seeing wild animals.

ADDITIONAL SKILL INSTRUCTION

CAUSE AND EFFECT Set up a tower of blocks on the floor. Roll a ball along the floor so that it knocks over the blocks. Invite children to describe what has happened and tell why it happened.

1. The blocks falling is what happened.
2. The ball rolling into the blocks is why it happened.

Help children discover a cause-and-effect scenario in this book. For example, on page 7, ask why the bear finds food (because he is hungry).

Name _____

Author's Purpose

Look at the picture and read the sentences.

Many trees live and grow in this forest.

Many animals live and grow in this forest.

Why do you think the author wrote about trees and animals?

The author wanted to tell what lives in a forest. The author wanted us to know that a forest is a home to many plants and animals.

Use the words in the box to fill in the blanks.

> show trees visit forest

1. The author likes the _____ .

2. The author wants to _____ that animals live in the forest.

3. The author wants others to _____ the forest.

4. The author likes to look at _____ .

54

Name _____

Vocabulary

Use a word from the box to complete each sentence.

Words to Know
around   find   food   grow   under   water

1. Look! The bear is in the _____ .

2. He hopes to _____ food there.

3. He likes to eat fish. Fish are his _____ .

4. Fish swim _____ the water.

5. The trees _____ tall.

6. The bear looks all _____ .

Learn About Worker Bees

SUMMARY Worker bees are responsible for making honey. In this book, readers follow a worker bee as it leaves the hive and visits flowers to collect nectar and pollen. The bee then returns to the hive, where other bees feed the pollen to young bees and turn the nectar into honey.

LESSON VOCABULARY

also	family
new	other
some	their

INTRODUCE THE BOOK

INTRODUCE THE TITLE AND AUTHOR Have children study the words and pictures on the book cover. Ask children if one of the words names the animal they see. Have children point to the picture and say *bee,* then point to the word *bee* on the cover and read it. Read the entire book title with the class, as well as the author's name. Let children share their ideas about or experiences with bees.

BUILD BACKGROUND Show children a jar of honey and encourage them to react to it. Then ask children if they know where honey comes from. If they don't know, explain that bees make honey. Speculate with children how bees might do this, and write their ideas on the board.

PREVIEW/TAKE A PICTURE WALK Encourage children to leaf through the book to become familiar with the pictures and the graphic elements. Have children pause on pages 4 and 5, and discuss the shape of the pictures and why the shape might be important. Also have children finger-trace the arrows, and ask them what they think these arrows represent. *(a sequence)*

READ THE BOOK

SET PURPOSE Ask children why they might want to read this book, and list their ideas. For example, some children might want to know why humans need bees. Encourage children to think of something that people get from bees.

STRATEGY SUPPORT: QUESTIONING Explain to children that asking questions while they read helps them better understand what they are reading. Model asking and answering questions about page 3: I wonder what the bees in the picture are doing? I read the text and it mentions that worker bees keep the hive working. The bees in the picture must be working on the hive.

COMPREHENSION QUESTIONS

PAGE 4 What is alike about the shape of the pictures and the shapes you see in the hive? What is different? *(Both shapes have six sides. The shapes of the pictures were made by people. The shapes in the hive were made by bees.)*

PAGE 5 What happens before the bees leave the flowers? What happens after? *(They get nectar and pollen. They return to the hive.)*

PAGES 6–7 Why do worker bees collect pollen and nectar? *(to feed new bees and to make honey)*

PAGES 3–8 What two things do worker bees do? *(They help make honey. They keep the hive working.)*

REVISIT THE BOOK

THINK AND SHARE

1. Responses will vary.
2. Possible response: Why do bees need honey? It helps me understand why they need to work.
3. *bees, feed*
4. The arrows show that the bee leaves the hive and flies to the flowers.

EXTEND UNDERSTANDING Review with children their initial thoughts and ideas about bees that they shared prior to reading. Ask children how their ideas about bees differ now that they've read the book. Prompt children to explain why bees visit flowers and how bees help people. Let children point to pictures in the book to support their ideas.

RESPONSE OPTIONS

WRITING Prompt children to write about the worker bee from the worker bee's perspective. Have children copy and complete this sentence and sentence starter: *I am a worker bee. I _____ .*

WORD WORK Write the word *work* on the board, and encourage children to share images or adjectives that come to mind when they hear this word. Ask children if they think the term *worker* is appropriate to describe the bee in the book. Encourage children to explain their ideas by describing what the bee does.

SCIENCE CONNECTION

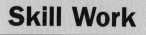

Speculate with children what would happen to the bees if no more flowers grew. Help children conclude that bees depend on the flowers. Ask: *Do the flowers depend on the bees?* Explain that bees help flowers to grow by taking pollen from flower to flower. Have children draw pictures of bees and daisies, then write titles for their pictures that explain this interdependency.

Skill Work

TEACH/REVIEW VOCABULARY

Give children sets of vocabulary word cards. Write each word on the chalkboard, then say the words in random order. Have children show each word as you say it.

ELL Show children a picture of an animal family, such as a dog with puppies. Write *family* on a self-stick note to place above the picture. Use the other vocabulary words to tell about the picture. Write and repeat the words, inviting children to say them with you. For example: This dog and her puppies are a *family*. The puppies are new. *Some* puppies have spots. *Their* fur is brown. This *other* puppy *also* has white spots.

TARGET SKILL AND STRATEGY

COMPARE AND CONTRAST Share with children that when they say how two things are *alike*, they tell how they are the same. When they say how two things are *different*, they tell how they are not the same. Have children *compare and contrast* the hive and the flowers on page 4. Ask: How are they alike? *(Bees spend time on both.)* How are they different? *(Flowers grow from seeds. Hives are built by bees.)*

QUESTIONING Remind children that forming questions while they read can help them remember what they are reading. Read pages 4–7 together. Have children come up with a question to ask about these pages. *(How do worker bees help their families?)*

ADDITIONAL SKILL INSTRUCTION

SEQUENCE OF EVENTS Review with children that a *sequence of events* is the order in which things happen. Have children turn to page 4, and ask them which part of the illustration helps explain a sequence of events. Confirm that the arrows point to what happens next. Invite children to explain in their own words what is happening in this picture. Continue discussing the sequence as shown on each page.

Name

Compare and Contrast

Think about how you are different from a worker bee. Write a word on the line that best fits each sentence.

Column A: You	**Column B: Worker Bees**
1. You live in a _____.	**2.** Worker bees live in a _____.
3. You leave your home to go _____ to _____.	**4.** Worker bees leave their hive to get _____.

5. Write one sentence that tells how you are similiar to a worker bee.

_____

_____

_____

Name_____

Vocabulary

Read the story. Think about the words in dark letters.
Then circle the letter of the answer to each question.

> Worker bees fly out of **their** hive. **Other** bees
> stay in the hive. They need to get **some** pollen
> from the flowers. They bring the pollen back to
> their **family** in the hive. The worker bees **also**
> help make honey.

1. What does the word **their** mean?

   a. belongs to it   **b.** belongs to them   **c.** belongs to you

2. What does the word **other** mean?

   a. different than   **b.** same as   **c.** one of

3. What does the word **some** mean?

   a. a lot of   **b.** not all of   **c.** all

4. What does the word **family** mean?

   a. two different animals   **b.** animals that live in a park
    c. a group of the same animals or plants

5. What does the word **also** mean?

   a. so   **b.** too   **c.** far

In My Room

SUMMARY In this fictional story, a young boy describes how his room at home looked when he was a baby, when he was three, and how it looks now. This illustrates for children how things, even our rooms, change over time.

LESSON VOCABULARY

always	become
day	everything
nothing	stays
things	

INTRODUCE THE BOOK

INTRODUCE THE TITLE AND AUTHOR Discuss with children the title and author of *In My Room*. Have children look at the cover art. Ask: What is the boy doing? What do you think this story will be about?

BUILD BACKGROUND Ask children to describe the room they sleep in at home. Some children may have their own bedroom, others may share their sleeping space with other family members. Ask children to tell how the room they sleep in looked when they were babies. How has it changed now that they are older?

PREVIEW/TAKE A PICTURE WALK As children preview the book, encourage them to look closely at the illustrations. Ask: Using the illustrations, what do you think happens in this story?

READ THE BOOK

SET PURPOSE Have children set a purpose for reading *In My Room*. Suggest that they think about something they want to learn. Think aloud: I see that the boy on the cover is playing with toys in his room. I wonder how his room looked when he was a baby? Did anything change as he grew older? I'm going to read and find out.

STRATEGY SUPPORT: SUMMARIZE After having children discuss and answer questions about the main idea of the story, guide them in summarizing the story. Use signal words first, next, and last to cue the children. Help children identify the key events and main idea in their summary of the story. Ask: What is this story about? What is the main thing that happens?

COMPREHENSION QUESTIONS

PAGE 3 How old was the boy when his room looked like this? (*The boy was a baby when his room looked like this.*)

PAGE 5 What did the boy's room have in it when he was three? (*The room had many things the boy could play with.*)

PAGE 7 What does the boy's room look like now that he is older? (*The room has games and books in it.*)

PAGE 8 What happened to the boy's old toys and books? (*The boy's younger sister plays with his old toys and books.*)

REVISIT THE BOOK

THINK AND SHARE

1. Possible response: Beginning – the room had a crib, a rocking chair, and baby toys; Middle – the room had a bigger bed, a teddy bear, and other toys; End – the room had books and games.
2. Possible response: The boy gets new games, toys, and books for his room. He gives his old games and books to his sister.
3. *everything; every* and *thing*
4. Possible response: Now his sister can play with the toys and read the books.

EXTEND UNDERSTANDING As the children read the story, ask them to pay close attention to what the boy's room looks like in each of the illustrations. Discuss how the illustrations help tell the story.

RESPONSE OPTIONS

WRITING Ask children to write about other ways they or their family may have changed since they were little. Perhaps they live in a different house or apartment, have new brothers and sisters, or have a pet.

SCIENCE CONNECTION

Suggest that children find out how their favorite animals change as they grow. Provide a selection of books and magazines relating to baby animals and their development. Encourage children to look for similarities and differences between how animal babies and human babies change.

Skill Work

TEACH/REVIEW VOCABULARY

Display the word *nothing* in a pocket chart. Read the word together. Then ask children to turn the pages of *My Room* and find the word. Read the sentence aloud. Ask children to think of another sentence that uses this word. Repeat for the other words. Display the vocabulary words on a word wall.

ELL Find and cut out pictures of items commonly found in a child's room, such as a bed, a lamp, a teddy bear, a doll, and so on. Help English language learners to identify and label these items. Say the word as you label the item, and ask children to repeat the word.

TARGET SKILL AND STRATEGY

SEQUENCE Remind children that *sequence* is the order in which things happen. Explain that the words *first, next,* and *last* are often used to tell about a sequence of events. Point out that the boy *first* describes the room when he was a baby. *Next,* he describes the room when he was three, and *last,* he describes his room now.

SUMMARIZE Remind children that when they read, they can use their own words to tell what happened in a story or book. As children read *In My Room,* encourage them to think about how they would describe the book to a friend who has not read it.

ADDITIONAL SKILL INSTRUCTION

AUTHOR'S PURPOSE Ask: Why do you think the author wrote this book? What did he want to make us think about?

Name_____

Sequence

Think about the things that you could do when you were a baby. Write them in the first box. Write the things that you could do when you were three in the second box. Write the things that you can do now in the third box.

1. When I was a baby, I could _____
_____
_____

↓

2. When I was three, I could _____
_____
_____

↓

3. Now, I can _____
_____
_____

4. Draw a picture of your room at home.

Name_____

Vocabulary

Read the words in the box. Write each word on the line.

Words to Know
always   become   day   everything
nothing   stays   things

1. day _____

2. nothing _____

3. become _____

4. things _____

5. always _____

6. everything _____

7. stays _____

Hank's Song

SUMMARY A bluebird, Hank, is frustrated because he cannot sing like his friend Jan. With practice and encouragement, he learns to appreciate his own unique singing voice.

LESSON VOCABULARY

any	enough
ever	every
own	sure
were	

INTRODUCE THE BOOK

INTRODUCE THE TITLE AND AUTHOR Discuss with children the title and the author of *Hank's Song*. Point out that the title includes the word *song;* ask children to name songs that they know.

BUILD BACKGROUND Invite children to tell about a time they learned to do something new. Ask: Did you learn all at once, or did it take practice? Encourage them to recall their feelings at the beginning of the process and describe how those feelings changed as their skills grew.

PREVIEW/TAKE A PICTURE WALK As children preview the book, encourage them to look closely at the illustrations. Ask: Based on the illustrations, what do you think will happen in this story?

READ THE BOOK

SET PURPOSE Help children set a purpose for reading *Hank's Song*. They might concentrate on the story's plot, compare its outcome to the predictions they made while looking at the illustrations, or just think about how they would describe the story to a friend.

STRATEGY SUPPORT: INFERRING Encourage children to use their knowledge to make an inference about Hank. Help them think about an idea about Hank based on the information in the story. Ask children why they made their conclusion about Hank. Have them use the illustrations and text in the book to help explain their reasoning.

COMPREHENSION QUESTIONS

PAGE 3 How does Hank feel at the beginning of the story? How can you tell? (*Hank feels sad; the illustration shows him frowning.*)

PAGE 5 What does the speech bubble on this page tell us? (*The speech bubble indicates that Hank is singing in a small voice like a mouse.*)

PAGE 6 What about this illustration is a clue that this story is make-believe? (*Hank is sitting on a bench that is just his size.*)

PAGE 7 What did Hank learn in this story? (*Hank learned to like the way he sings.*)

REVISIT THE BOOK

THINK AND SHARE

1. Possible response: Hank's Song—Rooster Song; My Song—Mary had a little lamb; Both songs are about an animal.
2. Hank feels sad. That guess helps me think that Hank will be sad at some point in the story.
3. *bluebird*; *blue*, *bird*
4. Responses will vary but should be about a trait of the reader.

EXTEND UNDERSTANDING As children read the book, ask them to think about whether Jan was a good friend to Hank. Ask: Did Jan help Hank? How? How would you have helped Hank?

RESPONSE OPTIONS

SPEAKING Ask children to summarize the story in their own words. Prompt children to use transition words such as *first, then*, and *finally* in their retelling.

WORD WORK Make a word-and-picture puzzle card for the compound word *bluebird*. Sketch a blue spot and a bird on one side of the card and print the word *bluebird* on the other. Show the picture to the children and have them guess the word. Turn the card over and read the word together. Then invite the children to make word-and-picture cards for other compound words.

SCIENCE CONNECTION

Help children use the Internet to locate the song of a real bluebird. Encourage them to compare the bluebird's song to those of other common birds.

Skill Work

TEACH/REVIEW VOCABULARY

Print each vocabulary word on a separate self-stick note. Read the words aloud with the children and talk about the definition of each word. Then ask volunteers to match the words on the self-stick notes to words in the book.

ELL Print the vocabulary words on word cards. Read them aloud, as a group. Then scatter the cards on the floor. Hand flashlights to one or two children. Call out a word from the list and let the children shine the flashlight on the corresponding word card.

TARGET SKILL AND STRATEGY

COMPARE AND CONTRAST Tell children: *Alike* means how things are the same. *Different* means how things are not the same. Draw two columns on the board labeled "Alike" and "Different." Then have children tell how birds and mice are alike and different. Write their answers in the appropriate column. After reading the story, see if children can add more responses to the columns.

INFERRING Remind children that *inferring* means making a guess based on information from the book. Tell children that they should guess what will happen based on what they read. Have children make an inference about Jan. What information did they use to make their guess?

ADDITIONAL SKILL INSTRUCTION

REALISM AND FANTASY Discuss the difference between realism and fantasy. A *realistic* story tells about something that could happen in real life. A *fantasy* is make-believe. Read page 3 together and ask: Could this happen in real life? Encourage children to look for examples of fantasy as they read.

Name _____

Compare and Contrast

We **compare** objects when they seem alike. We **contrast** objects when they seem different.

1-2. Draw a bluebird and a rooster in the box.

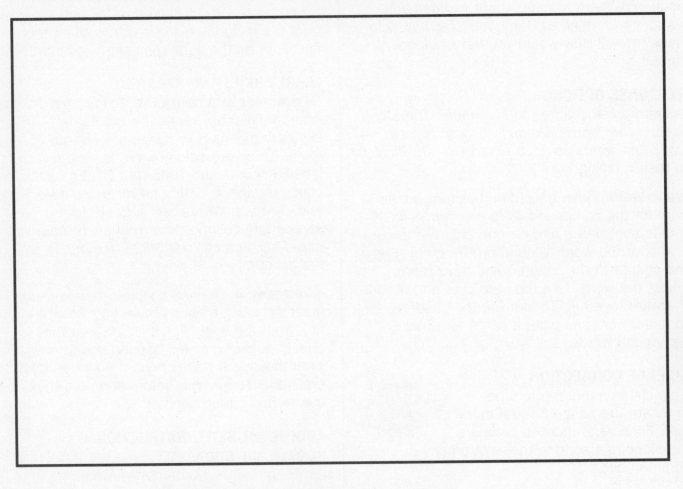

3. Write a sentence about how they are alike.

_____
- -
_____
- -
_____

Name _____

Vocabulary

Write a word from the box to complete each sentence.

Words to Know
any   enough   ever   every   own   sure   were

1. Hank and Jan _____ talking in the tree.

2. Jan said, "Almost _____ bluebird can sing like I do."

3. Hank asked, "Will I _____ learn to sing like Jan?"

4. Jan said, "If you practice _____, you can learn to sing."

5. Hank said, "Are you _____ ?"

6. Hank practiced _____ day.

7. In the end Hank liked his _____ song.

Gus the Pup

SUMMARY A family tells about their new pup Gus. They tell about what Gus does, what Gus needs, and what Gus likes to do.

LESSON VOCABULARY

away	car	friends
house	our	school
very		

INTRODUCE THE BOOK

INTRODUCE THE TITLE AND AUTHOR Have children study the book cover and explain what is happening in the picture. Ask children why the brown puppy is higher then the other puppies. Children might suggest that the puppies are playing. Invite children to read the book title with you. Also, read the author and illustrator's names. Ask children which puppy on the cover they think is Gus.

BUILD BACKGROUND Share with children that sometimes families make the decision to get a pet. Sometimes families must consider whether they are allergic to animals before choosing a pet. Other times, families must think about the kinds of animals they like. Talk to children about which pets a family might choose. If any children have pets, ask how their family chose that pet.

PREVIEW Invite children to preview the pictures in this book before they begin to read. Have children identify the people in the family and agree that the family consists of a father, a mother, a daughter, and a son. Tell children to turn to page 6 and guess what the puppy is doing in the picture.

READ THE BOOK

SET PURPOSE Guide children to set a purpose for reading. As they look at the book cover and think about the title, encourage them to voice what they would like to find out about this story. Jot down children's ideas. For example, perhaps children want to learn about what a puppy needs. Tell children to look for the answers to their questions as they read.

STRATEGY SUPPORT: MONITOR AND CLARIFY Mention to children that sometimes when they read, they form an idea about the text. When they reread the text, however, they may discover that they misunderstood what they read. Demonstrate monitoring and clarifying for the group. For example, read page 6 out loud, and then ask yourself, "Hmm, does Gus go to a school for children or a school for dogs?" Then read the text again, and say, "Ah! Gus goes to a school for dogs. I was able to clarify what I misunderstood, so now I understand it correctly."

COMPREHENSION QUESTIONS

PAGE 3 How does Gus get to the family's house? *(He rides in the car.)*

PAGE 5 Why are Gus's dishes on the floor? *(Possible response: so that he can reach them)*

PAGE 6 What is the man in the picture doing? *(Possible response: teaching Gus to not run away)*

PAGE 7 What ideas do you have about the theme after reading this page? *(Possible response: Puppies are nice pets and like to play.)*

REVISIT THE BOOK

THINK AND SHARE

1. Facts: Gus is a new pet, he needs dishes of food and water; Opinions: Gus is a good pet, he is very cute

2. Responses will vary.

3. Possible response: I would tell them that *very* means more than just *regular*.

4. People must feed their pets, train them, and take care of them.

EXTEND UNDERSTANDING On page 5, have children apply what they learn here to other pets they know about. *(All pets need food and water)* Speculate with children what other pets would eat. Ask: What would a lizard eat? What would a cat eat? and so on.

RESPONSE OPTIONS

WRITING Have children think of a pet and write it on their paper. Then have them write a list of three things they would need to do to take care of that pet. Tell children to use the information from the book or other ideas they have. You might have children copy and complete this sentence starter: To have a pet _____ you must _____.

VIEWING Let children look through books that show pictures of various pets. Encourage children to consider which of these pets might be the easiest to take care of. Then have them think about which of these pets would be the most difficult to take care of. Have children share ideas about these pets, based on the pictures in the books.

SCIENCE CONNECTION

Help children use the Internet to research unusual pets. Ask them to find the name of a pet, what it eats, and other things it needs to be happy and healthy. Have children share the information they find with their classmates.

Skill Work

TEACH/REVIEW VOCABULARY

Give children vocabulary word cards. Then write these sentences on the board: Some people live in a _____. Every day we go to _____. My parents drive a _____. People I like are my _____. The cat ran _____ from the dog. I like cookies _____ much. _____ school is called [name]. Read each sentence, and have children show the correct word that completes it.

ⒺⓁⓁ On the board, draw a house, a car, and your school building. Label each picture with its vocabulary word, and have children draw a group of children they know, and have them label these children as friends.

TARGET SKILL AND STRATEGY

FACT AND OPINION Help children understand the difference between facts and opinions. Facts are ideas that can be proven to be true. Opinions are ideas or feelings that people have. Ask children to look at page 3. The sentence *Gus is our new pup* is a fact. We could prove this by asking the family. Have children look again at page 4. The sentence *He is very cute!* is an opinion. We cannot prove that Gus is cute. The idea that he is cute is what someone thinks.

MONITOR AND CLARIFY Instruct children to pause after they read each page to consider what has happened so far in the story. To make sure they have understood everything correctly, tell children to reread the page and clarify any misconceptions.

ADDITIONAL SKILL INSTRUCTION

CAUSE AND EFFECT Hold up a sheet of paper and rip it. Say, "I ripped the paper. This is a cause. Now I have two pieces. This is an effect." Explain that what happened is the cause. Read page 3, and ask children to explain in their own words what happened (The family has a new pup Gus. Gus rides in the car to their house.) and why it happened (The family wanted a pet.). Have children use a cause-and-effect chart to keep track as they read *Gus the Pup*.

Name _____

Fact and Opinion

Dogs

Dogs are great pets. All dogs love to play ball and run outside. They need food and water to grow and be healthy. Some dogs have long fur and some dogs have short fur. They are the best kind of pet.

I. Read the sentences. Circle the opinions that are from the story.

They are the best kind of pet.

They need food and water to grow and be healthy.

All dogs love to play ball and run outside.

Some dogs have long fur and some dogs have short fur.

2. Write one fact from the story.

_____

- -

_____

- -

_____

Name _____

Vocabulary

Complete the letter with words from the box.
Some words have pictures to help you.

Words to Know
away   car   friends   house   our   school   very

Dear Carlos,   _____

We are getting a puppy! I am _____ happy.

The puppies are far _____ .

We will drive our _____ to get there.

I want my _____ to meet her.

She can't come to _____ .

Everyone can come to my _____ .

Please come to see _____ new puppy.

I will tell you more after we pick her up!

Your friend,

Mira

The Seasons Change

SUMMARY The weather outside is always changing. One reason why the weather changes is because of the different seasons. The weather begins to warm when it is spring, and the weather is mostly hot when it is summer. The weather begins to cool in the fall, and winter is the coldest time of all. This nonfiction text shows readers how the weather changes throughout the year.

LESSON VOCABULARY

afraid	again
few	how
read	soon

INTRODUCE THE BOOK

INTRODUCE THE TITLE AND AUTHOR Read the book title and author's name for the group. Point to each photograph and ask children to generate a list of words that describe the weather. Post the list in the classroom.

BUILD BACKGROUND Say the words *spring*, *summer*, *fall*, *winter* with the group, and ask children what these words stand for. Confirm that these words identify the seasons. Then invite children to talk about the seasonal weather where they live. Prompt discussion by asking, "How does it feel outside in the spring? in the summer? in the fall? in the winter?" Depending on where you live, you might explain that the change of the seasons and the weather can be more or less dramatic or obvious.

PREVIEW/TAKE A PICTURE WALK Invite children to begin looking through this book, and ask if they think this book will be a story or about something real. Ask children how they know, and agree that the photographs indicate that this book will tell them about something real; this book is nonfiction. Then have children study specific pages, and ask them to predict which season they will read about on that page. Ask: Which season will we read about on page 6? How do you know?

ELL Pretend to walk away from the group, waving. Ask children what you should say when you walk away or leave, and have them all say *good-bye* with you. Make other hand or body motions for other vocabulary words, such as nodding your head for *right* (correct), making a surprised face for *oh*, or stomping your foot with your hands on your hips for *won't*.

READ THE BOOK

SET PURPOSE As children study the book cover and think about the book's topic, ask them what they would like to learn from this book. Start a KWL chart and record the children's ideas in it. Encourage children to look for their ideas as they read. Complete the KWL chart after reading the book.

STRATEGY SUPPORT: VISUALIZE As children read *The Seasons Change*, prompt them to think about what the weather is like where they live in each season. As they read about a season, have them close their eyes and picture a typical day. Ask: What is the weather like? What do the trees look like? What birds and animals do you see? What kind of clothing are you wearing?

COMPREHENSION QUESTIONS

PAGE 5 Which season follows spring? *(summer)*

PAGE 6 What do you know about fall? How do the pictures confirm what you know? *(I know that leaves turn color in fall. The pictures show colorful leaves.)*

PAGE 7 How are trees in winter different from trees in fall? *(Trees in winter are bare. Trees in fall have colorful leaves.)*

PAGE 8 How do you think it would feel outside in the picture? *(It would feel cool and wet.)*

REVISIT THE BOOK

THINK AND SHARE

1. Responses will vary. Possible response: The author wrote this book to teach children the order of the seasons.

2. Possible response: I pictured playing in the snow and building a snowman in winter.

3. *good-bye*; 4 times

4. Possible responses: It is raining, so the sky is probably cloudy and gray.

EXTEND UNDERSTANDING Share with children that the seasons occur not only in sequence, but in a cycle. The cycle, or pattern, repeats over and over again. To demonstrate what you mean, draw four circles on the board that form a circle, like the quarter hour positions on a clock (12, 3, 6, and 9). Connect the circles with arrows pointing clockwise. In the top circle, write *spring*. Ask children which season would appear in the right circle. *(summer)* When complete, help children conclude that the cycle of the seasons occurs over and over again.

RESPONSE OPTIONS

WRITING Invite children to write about their favorite season. Write the following sentences on the board for children to copy to jump-start their ideas: *How does it feel outside? It is _____. It feels _____.* Have them add at least one more sentence about that season.

VIEWING Ahead of time, find pictures that represent the seasons. Hold up the pictures and give children a moment to study the details. Then ask children to identify which season they see. You might also mix up the photographs and have children put them in the correct order.

SCIENCE CONNECTION

Talk with children about the clothes they wear during different weather and seasons. Describe the weather, and have children supply what they would wear. For example: *It feels cold outside! It is snowing. I should wear _____.*

Skill Work

TEACH/REVIEW VOCABULARY

Write each word on an index card, and display the cards in random order. Say the words one at a time, and have children identify the correct word on the card. Work with children to use the words in context in sentences.

TARGET SKILL AND STRATEGY

AUTHOR'S PURPOSE Explain that an author's purpose is the reason why an author chose to write something. Speculate with children why the author might have chosen to write this book. Let children exchange ideas; for example, this author may want readers to learn about the seasons.

VISUALIZE Remind children that picturing a story or narrative in their minds as they read can help them remember details about what they are reading.

ADDITIONAL SKILL INSTRUCTION

DRAW CONCLUSIONS Remind children that they can think about what they already know about seasons and put those ideas together with those they learned from the book to make new decisions or understanding about seasons. You may use these steps to help children draw conclusions.

• First, discuss with children what this book was mostly about.

• Then ask children what new ideas they formed from reading this book.

Name_____

Author's Purpose

Look at the picture and read the sentences.

There are four seasons every year.
Changes in nature happen in each season.
The weather changes too.

Why do you think the author wrote this paragraph?

The author wanted to tell about the seasons changing. The author wanted us to know that things in nature and the weather change.

Use the words in box to fill in the blanks.

seasons	nature	tell

1. The author wants to teach about the _____ .

2. The author wants to _____ that the seasons change.

3. The author wants others to enjoy _____ .

74

Name_____

Vocabulary

Read the poem below, or listen as someone reads it to you. Look for the words from the box in the poem. Then circle the vocabulary words that you find in the poem.

Words to Know
afraid   again   few   how   read   soon

The Weather

You don't like winter weather?

Don't be afraid.

Soon it will be spring.

Leaves will grow.

Flowers will bloom.

How beautiful everything looks!

In a few weeks summer will come.

After that it will be fall.

Then winter comes again.

Stay inside and read a book!

Animals Change and Grow

SUMMARY This informational text describes how different animals grow and change over time. The book begins with the familiar animals, cat and dog, and then explores the growth and changes in others such as birds, gerbils, frogs, and butterflies.

LESSON VOCABULARY

done	know
push	visit
wait	

INTRODUCE THE BOOK

INTRODUCE THE TITLE AND AUTHOR Discuss with the children the title and author of *Animals Change and Grow.* Have children look at and identify the cover photographs. Ask: What do these pictures have in common with each other? What do you think you might learn about in this book?

BUILD BACKGROUND Engage children in a discussion of how they grow and change. Ask: How are you different now than two years ago? from when you were a baby? How do you think you might change in the future? If children have pets, ask how their animals have changed as well.

PREVIEW/TAKE A PICTURE WALK Have the children preview the book, looking at the pictures. Look specifically at the photographs on pages 4 and 5 and ask the children to describe what they see happening. Also encourage them to explore the other photographs and make predictions about the text.

READ THE BOOK

SET PURPOSE Based on your discussion of the cover photographs, invite children to share what about this text makes them interested in it. Ask: What animals would you like to learn about in this book? How do you think different animals grow and change?

STRATEGY SUPPORT: TEXT STRUCTURE Model for the children how to recognize the organization of written text. Ask children to tell what changes are shown on page 3. Also have them listen as you reread pages 4, 6, 7, and 8 aloud. Have children point out the sentence that is repeated on each of these pages. Help them to see the pattern that is repeated in the information about each animal.

COMPREHENSION QUESTIONS

PAGES 4–5 The text says that baby birds push out of eggs and later have feathers. Based on this information and photographs, do you think the birds can fly when they first come out of the eggs? Why or why not? *(No; Possible response: they need to wait until they grow feathers.)*

PAGE 6 How does the gerbil change over time? *(Possible responses: descriptions of size, closed/open eyes, amount of fur)*

PAGE 7 What are the different changes, in order, that this animal goes through? *(First, a tadpole; then it gets legs; last it changes into a frog.)*

PAGE 8 Look at the differences between each of these pictures. What does this tell you about the butterfly as it grows? *(Possible response: It goes through many different changes.)*

REVISIT THE BOOK

THINK AND SHARE

1. Possible response: A baby gerbil is not done growing. It is a fact because a baby gerbil has no fur and an adult gerbil has fur.
2. Pictures should mirror the photos on page 8.
3. *They, have*
4. It starts out as a tadpole, grows legs, and becomes a frog.

EXTEND UNDERSTANDING Call children's attention to the outside back cover of the book. Point out that this is a nonfiction book, meaning it contains factual information. Ask them to explain why this book is nonfiction, based on the information in the text. Also call attention to the "Science" label in the upper corner of the cover, and invite the children to share how this book is related to this content area.

RESPONSE OPTIONS

SPEAKING Ask children to describe the stages of a butterfly life cycle in their own words. Coach them in using the words *first*, *then*, and *last* to organize the sequence of events.

SCIENCE CONNECTION

Create a bulletin board. On one half, put the words *Animals change and grow* and invite the children to draw or help find photographs of baby and adult animals to put on the board. Label the other half of the board *We change and grow*. Invite the children to bring in two pictures of themselves: one current and one as a baby or younger child. Provide photos of yourself as well. Look at the board together and discuss the differences and changes you see in the pictures.

Skill Work

TEACH/REVIEW VOCABULARY

Create a set of cards with the vocabulary words printed on them. Create another set of cards with the following synonyms: *finished, understand, shove, stop by, stay.* Show each synonym card and read it aloud. Children can practice matching the correct words with the synonyms, saying the words as they do so.

TARGET SKILL AND STRATEGY

FACT AND OPINION Help children understand the difference between facts and opinions. Facts are ideas you can prove. Opinions are ideas that people think but cannot always be proven. Ask children to look at page 4. The sentence *Baby birds crawl out of eggs* is a fact. We can prove this by looking at other books about birds. Have children look at page 8. The sentence *Then it turns into a beautiful butterfly* is an opinion. We cannot prove that the butterfly is beautiful, the idea that it is beautiful is what someone thinks.

TEXT STRUCTURE Model for the children how to recognize the organization of written text. Using the information on page 8, assist children in writing the butterfly life cycle sequence in their own words, making sure to use the signal words *first*, *then*, and *last*. Have children go back and highlight or underline the signal words after they're done.

ADDITIONAL SKILL INSTRUCTION

SEQUENCE OF EVENTS Have the children turn to page 7 and look at the photographs. Ask them to describe what is happening as they refer to the photographs in sequence. Encourage them also to refer to the text for support.

ELL As you preview the book, invite English language learners to share the names of the young and adult animals in their home languages.

Name_____

Fact and Opinion

Read the story.

Pets

Pets are animals that live in a home with a family. Pets change as they grow. Kittens are pets that grow into cats. Puppies are pets that grow into dogs. Cats and dogs are the best kind of pets. Families love having pets!

---

1. Read the sentences. Circle the opinions that are from the story.

Kittens are pets that grow into cats.

Cats and dogs are the best kind of pets.

Pets change as they grow.

Families love having pets!

---

2. Write one fact from the story.

_____

_____

_____

Name_____

Vocabulary

Circle the word that best completes each sentence.
Write the word in the blank.

one   wait   know

_____

1. Do you _____ what a butterfly is?

visit   crawl   done

_____

2. You are not _____ growing yet.

push   wait   know

_____

3. If you _____ long enough, it will get bigger.

one   visit   know

_____

4. Children _____ their friends after school.

crawl   done   push

_____

5. Friends can _____ you on the swing
to go higher.

Ready for Winter?

SUMMARY This informational text describes the way some animals prepare for colder weather—migrating, growing thicker fur, seeking shelter, storing food.

LESSON VOCABULARY

before	does
good-bye	oh
right	won't

INTRODUCE THE BOOK

INTRODUCE THE TITLE AND AUTHOR Read the book title and author's name for the group. Ask children what they think the book is going to be about, based on the title and the picture on the cover.

BUILD BACKGROUND Ask children to think about some of the things they do differently when the weather becomes colder. Prompt them to remember that they wear warmer clothing and spend more time playing indoors. Point out that some animals do things to prepare for colder weather too. Ask them if they have seen groups of birds migrating or animals storing nuts and other food.

PREVIEW Invite children to preview the pictures in this book before they begin to read. Have children identify the animal or animals pictured on each page and ask them to predict what they might learn about the animals from reading this book.

READ THE BOOK

SET PURPOSE Help children set a purpose for reading, based on their own interest in animals. Encourage children to select a photo they might like to know more about.

STRATEGY SUPPORT: BACKROUND KNOWLEDGE Explain to children that they can use what they already know to help them understand what they read. Model text-to-self connections for page 3: This reminds me of a time last year when I saw a flock of geese flying overhead. Model for page 7: Sometimes I see chipmunks by my house that are busy gathering food for the winter.

COMPREHENSION QUESTIONS

PAGE 3 Where do some birds go in the fall? (*They fly to warmer places before it gets colder.*)

PAGE 5 What do some animals do to get ready for cold weather? (*Some animals grow new fur.*)

PAGES 6–7 What do other animals do in the fall? (*Some animals build new homes. Other animals find food.*)

PAGE 8 What season comes after fall? (*Winter comes after fall.*)

REVISIT THE BOOK

THINK AND SHARE

1. Possible response: gather food, build a new home, move to a warm place

2. Responses will vary.

3. warm; cold

4. Possible response: All of the animals make changes to get ready for colder weather.

EXTEND UNDERSTANDING Point out to children that some areas of the country are colder in fall and winter than other areas. They may find animals different from the ones pictured, depending on where they live. Work with children to research some of the animals that live near you to find out how they prepare for changing seasons.

SCIENCE CONNECTION

Point out that some animals use *camouflage* in the winter to protect themselves from other animals that might want to hurt them. A mule deer's coat changes from brown to gray to help it hide in a forest during the winter. An arctic fox's coat changes to white to help it blend into the snow in winter.

Skill Work

TEACH/REVIEW VOCABULARY

List the vocabulary words on the board or on chart paper: *before, does, good-bye, oh, right, won't.* Ask children to read, write, and spell each of the words. Print each word on an index card. Have children take turns choosing a card, reading the word, and using the word in a sentence of their own.

ELL Help children make cards with vocabulary words on one side and the translations in their home languages on the other. Place the cards with the translation facing up and have children capture cards by naming the vocabulary words.

TARGET SKILL AND STRATEGY

DRAW CONCLUSIONS After reading page 5, model this skill by asking: Why would fur help the fox in the cold? If necessary, ask children if they have ever felt fur, perhaps on a pet. Ask: What does fur feel like? How does fur help your pet?

BACKROUND KNOWLEDGE Mention to children that they can use what they already know to help them understand what they read. Have children use a KWL chart for *Ready for Winter* to generate questions for which they will look for answers as they read.

ADDITIONAL SKILL INSTRUCTION

COMPARE AND CONTRAST Remind children that when they compare two things, they tell how they are the same. When they contrast two things, they tell how they are different. Have children compare and contrast the bird on page 4 and the chipmunk on page 7. Ask: How are they alike? *(They are both collecting food.)* How are they different? *(The bird has feathers and the chipmunk has fur.)*

Name_____

Draw Conclusions

Use what you read in the book and what you already know to write answers to these questions.

1. Which word tells what a bird might do in the winter?

   _____

   -

   fly   swim   _____

2. Fur protects a fox from _____ .

   _____

   -

   heat   cold   _____

3. Look at page 6. What will the beaver do with the stick?

   _____

   -

   build   store   _____

4. Look at page 8. Are the animals ready for winter?

   _____

   -

   yes   no   _____

How do you know?

_____

- -

_____

- -

Name_____

Vocabulary

Read the words in the box. Write each word on the line.

Words to Know		
before	does	good-bye
oh	right	won't

1. good-bye _____

2. does _____

3. won't _____

4. before _____

5. oh _____

6. right _____

A Party for Pedro

SUMMARY Pedro's family is giving him a birthday party. They have a party that includes a piñata, tacos, and a band.

LESSON VOCABULARY

about	enjoy	gives
surprise	surprised	worry
would		

INTRODUCE THE BOOK

INTRODUCE THE TITLE AND AUTHOR Discuss with the children the title and the author of *A Party for Pedro*. Based on the title and the cover illustration, ask the children what special part of the party is shown. Talk about where the piñata game comes from and what that tells the reader about Pedro's family.

BUILD BACKGROUND Parties are a good way to learn about the music and food from different cultures. Ask the children to talk about different birthday parties they've been to and what was most fun about them. If they mention activities such as playing games together and eating special food, further the discussion by telling them they will be reading about one special birthday.

PREVIEW/USE TEXT FEATURES Invite children to look at the picture on page 7, and ask them what they think this book will be about. Then suggest they look through the rest of the book and figure out which character is Pedro. Ask: What do you think Pedro is celebrating?

READ THE BOOK

SET PURPOSE Most children will want to read about a party, but encourage children to set their own purpose for reading this story of Pedro's party. You can set the stage by stating that this is a story about a Hispanic family's birthday celebration. After the children have looked through the book, they should then be able to set a purpose for reading.

STRATEGY SUPPORT: MONITOR AND FIX UP Often, young readers think they are breaking the rules by going back to reread. Help children to understand that when you ask them questions and they don't know the answers, that's a clue that they should reread. It is important for them to realize that when they do not understand something they have a way for fixing it. This strategy will not only help the children's overall comprehension but also their ability to draw conclusions about what was important in Pedro's story. Remind the children that these strategies help them to think and read better.

COMPREHENSION QUESTIONS

PAGE 3 Why was the day special for Pedro? *(It was his birthday.)*

PAGE 5 What kind of game did the children play? *(a piñata game)*

PAGE 6 What food does Pedro's grandma make best? *(tacos)*

PAGE 8 Piñatas have been around what country for a long time? *(Mexico)*

REVISIT THE BOOK

THINK AND SHARE

1. Possible response: yes; he smiled and looked happy in the illustrations
2. Possible responses: You can reread, look at pictures, or keep reading to see if it makes sense.
3. Graphic organizer: birthday, wait, rain, plays, day
4. Grandma's candy, toys, treats

EXTEND UNDERSTANDING Have children turn to page 4. Point out the quotation marks, and remind children that such marks are used to show what a person actually said.

RESPONSE OPTIONS

SPEAKING Ask volunteers to prepare a short presentation of celebrations at their houses. They can include photographs, drawings, music, or any props in their presentations. Ask the audience to listen for similarities and differences.

SOCIAL STUDIES CONNECTION

Time For SOCIAL STUDIES

If possible, have any Hispanic children tell more about celebrations they have that mix their traditional culture with customs they know from their new country.

Skill Work

TEACH/REVIEW VOCABULARY

Write the vocabulary words on the board, say them, and ask the children to read them after you. Ask volunteers to use one or more vocabulary words in a sentence about parties. Repeat until all the words are used.

ELL Ask volunteers to tell about words in their home language that are good for describing parties and their activities. Encourage the children to describe parties in their home countries.

TARGET SKILL AND STRATEGY

DRAW CONCLUSIONS Model this skill by asking, after reading pages 3 and 4, "Why would Pedro ask if everything will be okay?" If necessary, prompt the children to remember that Pedro hopes to have a good birthday. Model a conclusion by saying, "It sounds as if Pedro hopes his birthday will be a good day."

MONITOR AND FIX UP It takes time for young readers to learn to monitor their understanding of what they are reading. One step in this process is to remind the children to use strategies, such as reread and review. Encourage them to ask themselves questions when they realize they didn't understand something. For example, they can ask themselves "Why doesn't this make sense?" Sometimes, they just need to continue and figure it out as they read.

ADDITIONAL SKILL INSTRUCTION

AUTHOR'S PURPOSE If children learn to ask why an author told a story a certain way or why the author put in some kinds of information, they will be closer to understanding what they are reading. In this story, ask why the author told about games, food, and music in Pedro's celebration. This way, the children will focus on how the author probably wanted to show this family's culture in the way they celebrate.

Name_____

Draw Conclusions

What reason best fits each sentence.
Put the letter of your answer at the beginning of each sentence.

_____

_____

_____ **1.** Pedro couldn't wait for this special day.

_____

_____

_____ **2.** Everyone loved the music.

_____

_____

_____ **3.** Pedro's Grandma makes a favorite food.

_____

_____

_____ **4.** Pedro was surprised by the box his mother gave him.

_____

_____

_____ **5.** Why was it a surprise to crack open the piñata?

A. Grandma's tacos are the best.

B. There were many toys inside.

C. Lots of treats fell out.

D. It was his birthday.

E. Everyone danced.

Name_____

Vocabulary

Read the story about Pedro. Put the word from the word box in the blank that best fits.

> ## Words to Know
>
> **about   enjoy   gives   surprise**
> **surprised   worry   would**

Pedro's story is _____ how

much he and his friends _____ his

party. Pedro does not _____ about

his family. They _____ all

_____ him and be there.

Pedro is _____ by all of the toys
inside the large box.

Space Star

SUMMARY A girl looks up at the night sky and dreams of traveling into space.

LESSON VOCABULARY

colors	draw
drew	great
over	show
sign	

INTRODUCE THE BOOK

INTRODUCE THE TITLE AND AUTHOR Discuss the title and author of *Space Star*. Based on the title and the picture on the cover, ask children to describe what they think this book might be about. Ask children to discuss what the girl on the cover might be drawing and why.

BUILD BACKGROUND Ask: Who has looked up at the sky at night? Discuss what children saw. Have them think about what it might be like to travel into space.

PREVIEW/TAKE A PICTURE WALK Invite children to take a picture walk to preview the text and pictures. Discuss who the people might be and what happens in each picture.

ELL Provide a web for children. In the center of the web, write the word *space*. Then have them write examples of different things found in space or related to space, such as stars, planets, moon, spaceship, rocket, shuttle. Children can also draw the different space-related objects or write the name of it in their home language next to the English word.

READ THE BOOK

SET PURPOSE Have children set a purpose for reading *Space Star*. Ask them to think about different meanings of the word *star*.

STRATEGY SUPPORT: VISUALIZE Encourage children to visualize, or picture in their minds, details of the story as they read. Explain that they can use details in the text to picture what they read and that visualizing in this way will help them understand and further enjoy all the stories they read. To help children visualize, read page 3 aloud. Then have them close their eyes and picture in their minds what Jean sees in the night sky. Then ask: Which details in the text help you picture what Jean sees in the night sky?

COMPREHENSION QUESTIONS

PAGE 3 What does Jean picture in her mind? Why? (*A spaceship. She wants to travel to the moon, stars, and planets.*)

PAGE 5 Why is there not enough room on the paper for Jean? (*Possible response: Because space is so big, and she wants to draw it bigger.*)

PAGE 7 Why does Jean smile when she draws her picture on the sidewalk? (*Possible response: Because she has finally drawn the picture she wanted to draw of her in space.*)

REVISIT THE BOOK

THINK AND SHARE

1. Possible responses: *Big Idea*: Jean has a dream of traveling in space. *What Jean Did*: Looked at the sky; Tried to draw her dream on paper; Tried to draw her dream on bigger paper; Drew her dream on the sidewalk.
2. Possible response: I pictured Jean flying in a spaceship in space. It helped me understand why this dream is so important to her.
3. Possible responses: I like to draw pictures with many *colors*. The *sign* helped us find our way to the park. She put the umbrella *over* our heads. We had to *show* Mom our clean hands.
4. Possible responses: Yes, I think she will live her dream because she seems very determined; No, I think she will grow up and have a new dream.

EXTEND UNDERSTANDING Invite children to discuss what it means to have a dream of doing something in the future. Ask volunteers to share something they dream about doing some day.

RESPONSE OPTIONS

ART Have children draw their own pictures of the night sky. If possible, let them use poster board or butcher paper so they can create big pictures, like Jean in *Space Star* did. If weather and space permits, give children sidewalk chalk and have them create their drawing outside on the playground.

SCIENCE CONNECTION

Provide children with a wide variety of books about space and space exploration. Have children choose a topic related to space—stars, a planet, the space shuttle, astronauts—and then explain in writing or in drawings three interesting facts about that topic. Have children share their work with the rest of the class.

Skill Work

TEACH/REVIEW VOCABULARY

Print the vocabulary words on index cards. Display each card and read the word aloud as a group. Hand out each card to a different child. Then have those children, one at a time, come to the board and lead the class in a game of hangman, using the word on the card. Once the class has figured out each word, have them say each letter and the word again as a class.

TARGET SKILL AND STRATEGY

THEME Remind children that every story has one "big idea," or meaning. Explain that as they read they can use something from their own lives to help them understand this "big idea." Ask: How does this story remind you of something that happened in your family?

VISUALIZE Explain to children that they can use their own experience and knowledge as they visualize. When possible, have them relate details in the selection to details they recall from their own experience. Say: As you imagine Jean drawing her picture on the sidewalk, how is it like a time you drew a picture on the sidewalk? What does the chalk feel like in your hand? What colors do you use?

ADDITIONAL SKILL INSTRUCTION

DRAW CONCLUSIONS Remind children that as they look at pictures and hear a story, they should think about what happens. They should use what they know to make up their mind about the characters in the story and what happens to them. Say: In the story, *Space Star*, Jeans seems very determined to draw a picture of herself in space. What does this tell you about Jean? *(Possible responses: That she really wants to travel in space; she likes to study space and the things in it.)*

Name _____

Theme

1. When you read *Space Star*, what do you learn about what Jean would love to do?

_____

- -

Jean wants to _____ .

_____

- -

2. Is there something you would love to do? _____
What would you love to do?

_____

- -

_____

_____

- -

_____

3. Draw a picture of yourself doing what you would love to do.

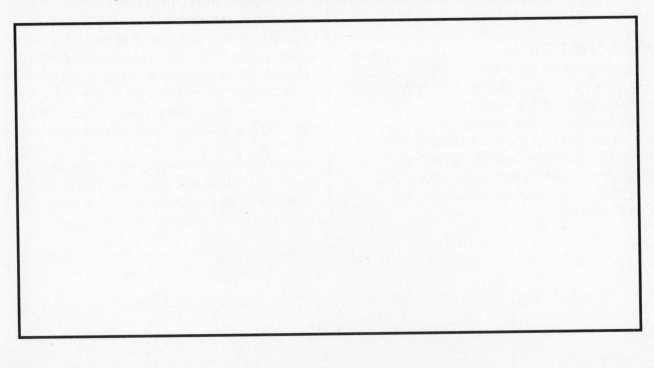

Name _____

Vocabulary

Write the word for each meaning on the lines.
Use the words in the box.

Words to Know

colors	draw	drew	great	over	show	sign

1. very good

   _____

2. to let someone see something

   _____

3. make a picture

   _____

4. red, yellow, blue

   _____

5. above

   _____

6. made a picture

   _____

7. something with a message on it

   _____

Our Leaders

SUMMARY This informational book explains the history of our nation's capital and the role it plays as the center of our government.

LESSON VOCABULARY

found	mouth
once	took
wild	

INTRODUCE THE BOOK

INTRODUCE THE TITLE AND AUTHOR Discuss with children the title and the author of *Our Leaders*. Focus children's attention on the content triangle on the cover. Ask: Why do you think this book is labeled *Social Studies*? What information might be included in this book? Turn to the title page and ask children to compare the text on this page to the text on the cover.

BUILD BACKGROUND Ask children to share what they might already know about Washington, D.C. Explain that Washington, D.C., is a city and the place where the President and other leaders of our country work.

PREVIEW/TAKE A PICTURE WALK Have children read the title and spend a few minutes looking at the illustrations and photos. Discuss what they suggest about the selection's content. Look at the picture of the White House on page 4. Ask: Do you know who lives in the White House?

READ THE BOOK

SET PURPOSE After children have previewed *Our Leaders*, ask them what question(s) they want to be able to answer after they read the book. Perhaps children can identify a picture they would like to learn more about.

STRATEGY SUPPORT: IMPORTANT IDEAS Tell children that good readers look for important ideas while they read. Authors will sometimes use captions and labels to show important ideas. Have children look at the photograph and read the caption. Ask: What important idea does this caption tell about? *(where our country's leaders work)*

COMPREHENSION QUESTIONS

PAGE 3 What does the sentence "Once this country was wild" mean? (*It means that there were once no houses or roads.*)

PAGES 4–5 Where was the city of Washington, D.C., built? (*It was built near the mouth of a river.*)

PAGES 6–7 What do the buildings in Washington, D.C., tell us? (*The buildings tell us about our past. They help us remember our leaders.*)

PAGE 8 What could you do if you visit Washington, D.C.? (*You could walk down the streets. You could think about the past and what is to come.*)

REVISIT THE BOOK

THINK AND SHARE

1. Our country's leaders needed a place to work.
2. Possible response: Washington, D.C. tells us about our past. Responses will vary.
3. Answers will vary. Sentences should reflect a correct understanding of what each word means.
4. Possible answer: to visit the White House; to learn about our leaders; to see important buildings; to learn about our past

EXTEND UNDERSTANDING After reading, have children go back and look at the illustrations and photographs. Ask: How does each illustration or photograph help you understand what is happening in the text?

RESPONSE OPTIONS

WRITING Ask children to imagine planning a visit to Washington, D.C. Invite them to write a few sentences describing what they would do and see on their visit.

SOCIAL STUDIES CONNECTION

Time For SOCIAL STUDIES

Have on hand a map of the United States. Help children locate their own state on the map. Then help them locate Washington, D.C. Provide a selection of nonfiction books and help children use the Internet to learn more about Washington, D.C.

Skill Work

TEACH/REVIEW VOCABULARY

Write the word *found* on a sentence strip. Ask: What does *found* mean? Turn to page 6 and ask a volunteer to find the sentence containing the word. Read the sentence together, and talk about the meaning of the word in context. Repeat this exercise for the words *mouth*, *once*, *wild*, and *took*.

ELL Print each vocabulary word on an index card. Stack the cards face down in a pile. Have children take turns picking a card and making up a riddle for the word for others to guess. Riddles might include: *The word starts with the letter _____; This word means the opposite of _____.*

TARGET SKILL AND STRATEGY

FACTS AND DETAILS Help children understand that *details* are small pieces of information. *Facts* are pieces of information that can be proven to be true. Facts and details can help readers picture in their minds, or visualize, what they read. Ask children to look at page 3. The sentence "Leaders make a country strong" is a *detail*. Have children look at page 5. The sentences "People called the new city Washington, D.C. It was named after our first President" are *facts*. It is true that Washington, D.C., was named after George Washington.

IMPORTANT IDEAS Have children look at the labels and photographs on page 7. Ask: What important idea do these labels and photographs tell us about? *(Possible response: other important buildings our leaders work in)* Encourage children to think of buildings people they know, such as principals and doctors, work in. Ask: What kinds of pictures and labels would show these types buildings? *(Possible responses: school; hospital)*

ADDITIONAL SKILL INSTRUCTION

CAUSE AND EFFECT Remind children that when they read, they can think about what happened and why it happened. Turn to page 4. Read the paragraph and ask: Why was the city built? Guide children to understand that the city was built because the leaders needed a place to work.

Name _____

Facts and Details

A *detail* is a piece of information about a story. A *fact* is a piece of information that can be proven to be true.

Read the story.

> ### A Visit to Washington, D.C.
>
> My family had a great time in Washington, D.C. The cherry trees were in bloom. We liked the Washington Monument. The White House is in Washington, D.C. It was fun to see where the President lives.

I. Read the details. Circle the details that are from the story.

Washington, D.C., is a big city.

The cherry trees were in bloom.

We took a plane to Washington, D.C.

We liked the Washington Monument.

2. Write one fact about the story.

_____

- -

_____

- -

_____

- -

_____

Name _____

Vocabulary

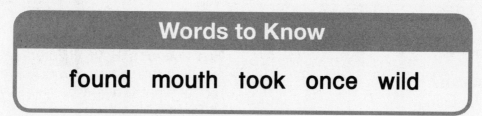

Words to Know

found   mouth   took   once   wild

Find each word from the box and circle it.

```
X  H  Y  P  W  V  T  I  L
L  M  O  U  T  H  O  N  I
D  N  H  G  G  D  O  E  H
V  H  D  L  T  N  K  M  J
O  T  C  B  C  Q  D  C  F
N  N  M  A  U  W  X  K  N
C  L  K  K  B  U  R  X  D
E  V  V  F  O  U  N  D  H
F  T  O  C  P  W  I  L  D
```

Grandma's Farm

SUMMARY A boy visits his grandma's farm and helps her do her work.

LESSON VOCABULARY

above	moon
eight	touch
laugh	

INTRODUCE THE BOOK

INTRODUCE THE TITLE AND AUTHOR Discuss the title and author of *Grandma's Farm*. Based on the title and the picture on the cover, ask children to describe what they think this book might be about. Ask children to discuss the different animals and buildings they see on the cover of the book.

BUILD BACKGROUND Invite children to discuss any experiences they have with farms, farm animals, or farm products. Discuss what children might see on farm, such as animals, buildings, machinery, and so on. Have children think about products they use that come from a farm, such as milk and eggs.

PREVIEW/TAKE A PICTURE WALK Invite children to take a picture walk to preview the text and pictures. Discuss who the people might be and what is happening in each picture.

ELL Provide a web for children. In the center of the web, write the word *farm*. Then have them write examples of different things found on a farm and different products from a farm, such as chickens, pigs, cows, milk, and eggs. Children can also draw the different farm-related objects or write the name of it in their home language next to the English word.

READ THE BOOK

SET PURPOSE Have children set a purpose for reading *Grandma's Farm*. Ask them to think about what it might be like to visit or live on a farm.

STRATEGY SUPPORT: QUESTIONING During reading, encourage children to ask questions about the text. Remind them that asking questions can help them better understand what they are reading. For example, model on page 4: I wonder kinds of things the boy does on the farm?

COMPREHENSION QUESTIONS

PAGE 3 Does the boy enjoy visiting Grandma's farm? How do you know? *(Yes; he says he has the best time visiting Grandma's farm.)*

PAGE 5 How does the boy help Grandma with the horses? *(He feeds them.)*

PAGE 6 Has Grandma lived on a farm for a long time? How do you know? *(Yes; she tells the boy funny stories about when she was a girl on the farm.)*

REVISIT THE BOOK

THINK AND SHARE

1. Fact: I visit for eight weeks. Details: do farm work, feed horses, hear stories, see the stars.
2. Answers will vary.
3. The word is *above*. Possible response: The bowls are in the cabinet above the sink. Another word that means the opposite of below is *over*.
4. Possible responses: If I visited a farm, I would like to milk a cow and ride a horse.

EXTEND UNDERSTANDING Invite children to discuss what it would be like to visit a farm. Encourage them to use all of their senses to describe what the experience might be like for them. For example, have them think about what they might smell.

RESPONSE OPTIONS

ART Have children think about what it would be like if they owned a farm. What animals would they like to have? What kind of farm machinery would they have? Have children draw a picture of their farm and write a caption for it.

SOCIAL STUDIES CONNECTION

Provide children with a wide variety of books about farms and farm products. Help children to understand the importance of farms and farming to their community. Have children identify products they use that come from farms, such as eggs, flour, meat, milk. Then have them explain in writing or in drawings why farms are important to everyone. Have children share their ideas with the rest of the class.

Skill Work

TEACH/REVIEW VOCABULARY

List the vocabulary words on the board or on chart paper: *above, eight, laugh, moon, touch.* Ask children to read, write, and spell each of the words. Print each word on an index card. Have children take turns choosing a card, reading the card, and finding the word in the book.

TARGET SKILL AND STRATEGY

FACTS AND DETAILS Explain to children that *details* are small pieces of information. *Facts* are pieces of information that can be proven true. Both the text and pictures may give details. Have children look for a detail on page 5 that helps them understand what horses eat. *(the picture shows the boy feeding hay to the horses)*

QUESTIONING Explain to children that when they read, it helps to ask questions about the text. Asking questions helps clarify information or parts of a story. For example, for this story, children might ask: "Why can't the boy ride the horse now?" *(The boy is probably too small to ride the horse.)*

ADDITIONAL SKILL INSTRUCTION

DRAW CONCLUSIONS Remind children that as they look at pictures and hear a story, they should think about what happens. They should use what they know to make up their mind about what the story is all about. Say: In the story *Grandma's Farm*, the boy loves to visit Grandma's farm. What might this tell you about the boy? *(Possible responses: That he loves animals or that he likes to spend time with his grandma.)*

Name _____

Facts and Details

Think about what you read in *Grandma's Farm*.
Circle the answer to the question.

1. What is a detail about horses from the story?

   a) We laugh a lot.

   b) I know how to feed them.

   c) I can touch the eggs.

   I love to do work on Grandma's farm.

2. What detail tells more about this sentence?

   a) I love to hear about the farm.

   b) We see the moon and stars above.

   c) I can touch the eggs.

3. Draw a picture of something you might see on a farm.

Name _____

Vocabulary

Pick a word from the box to finish each sentence.
Write the word on the line.

Words to Know
above   eight   laugh   moon   touch

1. This year, Dylan will be _____ years old.

2. Mom and I _____ at Dad's jokes.

3. "Don't _____ the cakes," said Grandma.

4. We looked for the _____ in the night sky.

5. Grandpa put the cookies _____ the counter so we could not reach them.

A New Baby Brother

SUMMARY A young boy worries about the arrival of a new baby but ends up liking being a big brother.

LESSON VOCABULARY

picture   remember
room   stood
thought

INTRODUCE THE BOOK

INTRODUCE THE TITLE AND AUTHOR Discuss with children the title and author of *A New Baby Brother*. Based on the title, what do children think the story might be about? Who might the big brother in the story be?

BUILD BACKGROUND Encourage children to discuss any experience they have with the arrival of a new sibling. If they don't have personal experience, suggest they imagine how they would feel if they got a new baby brother or sister.

PREVIEW Before reading, have children look at the pictures in the book. Who do they think the people in the story are? What are the people doing?

ELL Check children's understanding of such words as *thought* and *remember*. Discuss the meanings of the words, giving examples of each in a sentence. Then have children give their own examples.

READ THE BOOK

SET PURPOSE Have children set a purpose for reading *A New Baby Brother*. Help prompt a purpose by exploring the following: What do children hope to find out about the family on the cover? Why is the book called *A New Baby Brother*?

STRATEGY SUPPORT: STORY STRUCTURE During reading, encourage children to notice how events in the story are arranged in an order from beginning to end. Each thing that happens in a story leads to the next thing. When they think about how all these events fit together, they can tell what the story is all about.

COMPREHENSION QUESTIONS

PAGES 4 AND 5 Think about the questions Marco is asking. Why is he asking them? *(Possible response: He is worried about the new baby changing everything.)*

PAGE 6 How do you think Marco feels about sharing his room? *(Responses will vary.)*

PAGE 7 How does Marco feel about the baby at the end of the story? *(Possible response: He likes the baby.)*

REVISIT THE BOOK

THINK AND SHARE

1. Possible responses: Changes can ge good. Marco learns that he's good at being an older brother.
2. Possible response: Beginning: Marco is going to have a baby brother. Middle: Marco is worried that having a baby brother will change everything. End: Marco likes being a big brother.
3. Sentences will vary.
4. Responses will vary.

EXTEND UNDERSTANDING Discuss how every-thing in this story could really happen. Then invite children to think of ways to turn this into a make-believe story. Help them to make sure the new story has a beginning, middle, and end.

RESPONSE OPTIONS

VIEWING Point out the family picture on the cover of *A New Baby Brother*. Then, have children draw their own family picture.

SOCIAL STUDIES CONNECTION

Display books that show a variety of family types (single parent, many children, single child, adoptive families, extended families, etc.). Give children the opportunity to look through the books and talk about the different kinds of families they see.

Skill Work

TEACH/REVIEW VOCABULARY

Write the vocabulary words on index cards. Have children take turns choosing cards and then using the word in a sentence.

TARGET SKILL AND STRATEGY

THEME Explain to children that the *theme* is the "big idea," or meaning, of the story. Events that happen at the beginning, middle, and end of a story can help readers uncover the theme. Ask: If Marco was unhappy about having a baby brother at the end of the story, how would that change the theme? *(Possible response: The theme would be that not all changes are good ones; Not everyone is happy with changes.)*

STORY STRUCTURE Remind children that each thing that happens in a story leads to the next thing that happens. Together, these things show what the story is about. Tell children that if they keep track of the impor-tant things that happen in the story, they will learn more about the characters and where and when the story takes place. They will also be able to tell the plot of the story since they have followed it from beginning to end.

ADDITIONAL SKILL INSTRUCTION

REALISM AND FANTASY Ask children if a story where a boy finds a coat that makes him invisible is real or make-believe. Ask: Could this really happen? Have children explain their answers. Invite children to give you examples of stories where make-believe things happen. Then, ask children if a story where a boy finds a coat, returns it to its owner, and gets a reward is real or make-believe. Ask: Could this really happen? Have children explain their answer. Tell children that as they read, they should decide if the story could really happen or if it is make-believe. After reading, discuss their opinions.

Name _____

Theme

In the boxes below, draw something that happened in the beginning, middle, and end of *A New Baby Brother*. Then write a sentence about the "big idea" of the story.

Beginning

Middle

End

_____

_____

_____

Name _____

Vocabulary

Find the following hidden words. Words can go across or down.
When you have found a word, write it on the line below the puzzle.

Words to Know

picture	remember	room	stood	thought

```
J H Y P O T E T J Y E C W Y
K L O I C R Y R M M S L U P
S A R C D L K T H O U G H T
D J I T E U D M Y P S P C R
T L O U Y A N D P O T Y F I
A P P R E L R E M E O T E R
I L T E T A N T Y P O R O M
T Y L V T Y I L E V D M K I
R E M E M B E R I S H A N E
K I U L S T R O O Z P I C T
U V W J A V I R O O M Y P L
```

1. _____

2. _____

3. _____

4. _____

5. _____

My Babysitter

SUMMARY This nonfictional reader tells the story of a boy whose mother has to go to work and leave him with a babysitter. At first, he is unsure about the sitter and doesn't believe the sitter will know what to do. But his mother reassures him that the babysitter is good, that he will have fun, and that she will return home soon.

LESSON VOCABULARY

across	because
dance	only
opened	shoes
told	

INTRODUCE THE BOOK

INTRODUCE THE TITLE AND AUTHOR Ask children to look at the front cover of the reader. Read with them the title of the book and the author's name. Ask what they think the book is going to be about, based on the title and picture on the cover.

BUILD BACKGROUND Ask children if they have ever had a babysitter. If they have, ask them if they liked their babysitters and why. If they haven't, ask them if they think it would be nice to have a babysitter. Also, ask children to name some of the reasons why parents sometimes need to hire babysitters.

PREVIEW/ILLUSTRATIONS Invite children to open the book and take a *picture walk* through the book. Then ask: Does this story look like it could really happen? Also ask: Who do you think are the main characters in the story? Ask the children to explain what clues led them to their answers.

READ THE BOOK

SET PURPOSE After children have previewed the book, ask them what question(s) they want to be able to answer after they read the book. Ask if there are any questions they have about the characters in the story.

STRATEGY SUPPORT: PREDICT/CONFIRM PREDICTIONS Predicting helps children set a purpose for reading and make sense of the text. As children make predictions about the book, encourage them to give reasons for their predictions. Remind them to use what they already know to make their predictions. Then have them confirm whether their predictions were accurate.

COMPREHENSION QUESTIONS

PAGE 3 Why does the boy's mom have to leave? *(She has opened a store and has to go to work.)*

PAGE 3 Where does the babysitter live? *(across the street)*

PAGE 4 What is the boy worried about? *(He is worried that the babysitter won't know how to take care of him.)*

PAGE 5 Why does the boy want to put on his shoes? *(He wants to go with his mom rather than stay at home with a babysitter.)*

PAGE 6 Why does the boy change his mind about the babysitter? *(His mom tells him the babysitter will play any game he wants.)*

REVISIT THE BOOK

THINK AND SHARE

1. His mom is going to work.
2. Possible response: I thought the book might be about a boy who was worried about having a babysitter. I was right.
3. Responses will vary. She started a new business.
4. It can be fun.

EXTEND UNDERSTANDING Discuss with children the use of thought bubbles in illustrations. Direct children to the cover illustration, and emphasize how much information can be communicated through pictures. Have children interpret again what the cover illustration is conveying.

RESPONSE OPTIONS

SPEAKING Invite children to tell a story from their own lives that includes a cause and effect. Explain that the word *because* might be helpful. Give the children an example from your own life. (Example: I walked to school today because the weather was nice.)

SCIENCE CONNECTION

Develop an in-class science project that shows cause and effect. One possibility is to plant seeds, water them, give them light, and monitor the plants' growth. Ask students to list the causes and the effect.

Skill Work

TEACH/REVIEW VOCABULARY

Write the vocabulary words on the board. Help children find the words in the book. Guide them in reading the sentences that contain the words, and ask children to tell what they think each word means.

ELL Ask English language learners to write the vocabulary words on homemade word cards. Encourage them to write the word in their home language, if it will aid their comprehension. Then ask the children to draw pictures to illustrate what they mean on the other side.

TARGET SKILL AND STRATEGY

CAUSE AND EFFECT Explain to children that a *cause* is something that happens, and an *effect* is something that happens as a result of the cause. (Examples: Cause: You spend the whole day playing in the hot sun; Effect: You get a sunburn. Cause: There is a very bad snowstorm; Effect: There is a "snow day" and school is cancelled.) Ask children to draw a line down the middle of a sheet of paper. Then ask them to draw one picture on each side of the line: one picture for the cause and one for the effect. Invite children to draw pictures of something that has happened to them or someone they know.

PREDICT/CONFIRM PREDICTIONS Point out to children that as they read, it is a good idea to think about what might happen next in the story. Turn to page 4. The children will see that the boy is worried about his babysitter. Ask them to predict what might happen when the boy meets the babysitter. After they have finished the story, ask whether their predictions were accurate.

ADDITIONAL SKILL INSTRUCTION

MAIN IDEA Remind children that the main idea of a book is the most important thing the author wanted them to learn from the book. After reading the book, guide children in identifying the main idea.

Name _____

Cause and Effect

The sentences on the left tell a **cause**.
The sentences on the right tell an **effect**.
Draw a line to match each cause with its effect.

I. A mom goes to work.

2. It is time for a nap.

3. Mom comes home from work.

4. It is lunchtime.

5. You asked the babysitter to play a game.

a. The babysitter leaves.

b. The babysitter makes lunch.

c. A babysitter is coming to stay.

d. The babysitter tucks you into bed.

e. The babysitter plays a game.

Name _____

Vocabulary

Say each word aloud to count the number of syllables. Write that number on the line.

1. across   How many syllables?_____

2. because   How many syllables?_____

3. dance   How many syllables?_____

4. only   How many syllables?_____

5. opened   How many syllables?_____

6. shoes   How many syllables?_____

7. told   How many syllables?_____

8. Draw a picture of a person walking *across* something.

What Brown Saw

SUMMARY In this story, a dog observes how different animals gather food.

LESSON VOCABULARY

along	behind
eyes	never
pulling	toward

INTRODUCE THE BOOK

INTRODUCE THE TITLE AND AUTHOR Discuss with children the title and author of *What Brown Saw*. Also have children look at the picture on the cover. Ask what they think the book is going to be about based on the title and picture on the cover.

BUILD BACKGROUND Ask children to share what they know about how animals get food. Ask: Have you ever seen squirrels or birds gather food? How do they do it?

PREVIEW/TAKE A PICTURE WALK Have children look at the pictures in the book before reading. Ask: Who is the story about? Where does the story happen? Where does the story begin? Where does it end? Have children read the heading for the background information on page 8. Ask and discuss: Is this part of the story? What is this part of the book about? Why did the author include this information?

READ THE BOOK

SET PURPOSE Have children set a purpose for reading *What Brown Saw*. Remind children of what they discussed when the title, author, and cover art were introduced. You may need to work with children to have them set their own purpose. Ask: Would you like to know what Brown was watching?

STRATEGY SUPPORT: MONITOR AND CLARIFY Make available a children's dictionary so that children can look up unfamiliar words as they read. Think aloud as you model using the dictionary: I'm not sure what *toward* means. I think I'll look it up in a dictionary.

ELL Give each child a two-column problem/solution chart. In the Problems column, list the following: hungry squirrel, hungry ant, hungry bird, hungry dog. For each problem, have children draw the food that was the solution for each animal in the story.

COMPREHENSION QUESTIONS

PAGE 3 On this page, Brown is talking to you, the reader. Do you think that could really happen or is it make-believe? Why? (*It is make-believe because dogs can't talk in real life.*)

PAGE 4 Where was the squirrel? (*in Brown's yard behind the house*)

PAGES 4–6 Which animal did Brown see first, next, and last? (*First: squirrel, next: ant, last: bird*)

PAGES 4–7 Which picture is the most like real life? Why? (*Possible response: The picture on page 7 because it looks like the way a dog eats food. In the other pictures, the squirrel has too many nuts, the ant is too big, and the bird is carrying an apple as big as it is.*)

PAGE 7 Draw a picture of how the character Brown felt at the end of the story. (*Picture should depict Brown as being happy.*)

REVISIT THE BOOK

THINK AND SHARE

1. Brown, a squirrel, an ant, a bird; This story is about what Brown sees in the yard.
2. Responses will vary.
3. the ant
4. Possible response: People give Brown food. The other animals must get their own food.

EXTEND UNDERSTANDING Turn children's attention to the background information on page 8. Ask: How do plants in the story help the animals? How do the animals in the story help the plants? Guide children to see that the fruit and nuts in the story are parts of plants, and that they have seeds that are dropped when the animals eat them.

RESPONSE OPTIONS

SPEAKING Form groups of three children. Have each member choose a character other than Brown from the story. Have each child say what he or she thinks his or her character might say about finding food. The character should talk about why it wants food, what kind of food it wants, how it will find the food, and what it will do with the food.

SCIENCE CONNECTION

Display books and other information about food chains. Have children draw the steps of any food chain that interests them. For example, they might illustrate worm-fish-bear or grass-zebra-lion. Lead children in a discussion of how animals get food from their habitat.

Skill Work

TEACH/REVIEW VOCABULARY

Give each child a set of vocabulary cards. Act out the following sentences as you say them aloud, replacing each vocabulary word by saying *blank:* These are my (eyes). I am (pulling) the chair. I am walking (along) the wall. I am (behind) the desk. I am walking (toward) the door. You should (never) be mean. Have children hold up the word that completes each sentence.

TARGET SKILL AND STRATEGY

CHARACTER, SETTING, AND PLOT Tell children that *characters* are people or animals in stories. Then say that the main character in *What Brown Saw* is Brown. Also, ask children to think about the places they see in the pictures. This is called the *setting*. The *plot* is all events that happen in a story from beginning to end. Have children retell the plot of *What Brown Saw*.

MONITOR AND CLARIFY Remind children that what they read should make sense. When they encounter a word they don't know, finding out what the word means can help them understand what they read. They can look up the word in the dictionary.

ADDITIONAL SKILL INSTRUCTION

REALISM AND FANTASY Remind children that a realistic story tells about something that could happen in real life. A fantasy is make-believe. Ask: Is *What Brown Saw* a realistic story or a fantasy? Have children explain their reasoning.

Name _____

Character, Setting, and Plot

In the boxes below, draw something that happened in the beginning, middle, and end of *What Brown Saw*. Under each picture, write a sentence about who is in the picture and what they are doing.

Name _____

Vocabulary

Draw a line to match each word with the word or words that mean the same.

1. along   a. things to see with

2. behind   b. not at all

3. eyes   c. after

4. never   d. together

5. Write a sentence that uses the words *pulling* and *toward*.

_____
- -
_____
_____
- -
_____
_____
- -
_____

Fly Away Owl!

SUMMARY This fiction book is about a boy who finds a hurt owl in his yard. The owl is taken to a shelter to get better and then is released back into the wild.

LESSON VOCABULARY

door	loved
should	wood

INTRODUCE THE BOOK

INTRODUCE THE TITLE AND AUTHOR Discuss with children the title and the author of *Fly Away Owl!* Encourage them to describe what they see happening on the front cover. Ask: What type of bird is this? What are the people doing? Why do you think they are waving and where do you think the owl is going? How does this illustration relate to the title, *Fly Away Owl!?*

BUILD BACKGROUND Engage children in a discussion of animals and animal shelters. Have them share what they know about animal shelters and what shelters can do for animals. Ask: How do shelters help animals? Have you ever taken an animal to a shelter? Why? Have you ever adopted an animal from a shelter?

PREVIEW/TAKE A PICTURE WALK Have children preview the book by flipping through the pages and looking at the illustrations. Invite them to describe what they see happening on each page and make predictions about the text. Ask: What do you think happened to the owl? What is the boy doing? What is the woman doing with the owl? What do you see happening at the end?

READ THE BOOK

SET PURPOSE Before reading, guide children in setting a purpose for reading the book. Based on your preview of the illustrations, invite children to share what is most interesting to them about the book. Encourage them to share which picture they like best as well as what they would like to know more about. Ask: Why do you want to know more about this illustration? What do you think is happening here? Let's read to find out.

STRATEGY SUPPORT: BACKGROUND KNOWLEDGE Remind children that using what they already know when they read can help them better understand a story. Have children discuss what they would do if they found an injured animal. Encourage them read to find out if the boy in the story does the same thing.

COMPREHENSION QUESTIONS

PAGE 3 Where did the boy find the owl? *(in his yard by the wood)*

PAGE 4 Why did the dad call the animal shelter? *(The owl was hurt and a shelter takes care of hurt animals.)*

PAGE 5 Why do you think the woman put the owl in a cage? *(Responses will vary: So it wouldn't get away, so it would stay safe, so she could help it.)*

PAGE 6 What do owls like to eat? *(mice)*

PAGE 8 Why do you think they let the owl go back into the wild? *(The owl was originally from the wild, that's where it lives; it is better for an owl to be in the wild than in a shelter.)*

REVISIT THE BOOK

THINK AND SHARE

1. The owl was let go because it is a wild animal.
2. Responses will vary but should show an understanding of animal shelters.
3. Responses should show understanding of word definitions as well as proper usage and context.
4. Responses will vary. Make sure children give reasons for their answers.

EXTEND UNDERSTANDING Explain to children that a *setting* is where a story takes place, and that a story can also have more than one setting. Have children look back through the book to determine the settings in the book. *(yard, shelter, forest)* Have children describe the settings and explain why each is important to the events in the book.

RESPONSE OPTIONS

WRITING Assist the children in writing a short retelling of the story, making sure to include the main events from the book. Use signal words such as *first*, *next*, and *last* to help children organize their ideas. Then children may illustrate their writing.

SOCIAL STUDIES CONNECTION

Talk with children about animal shelters or rescue associations and what they do. Discuss how these organizations help animals and are important to our society. If possible, invite someone from an animal shelter or rescue association to come speak to the class about the work they do. Children may also enjoy participating in a community service activity to benefit the shelter, such as gathering food, blankets, or other necessary items.

Skill Work

TEACH/REVIEW VOCABULARY

Have children practice writing each of the vocabulary words on their own paper. Use each word in a sentence for the children and then help them write their own sentences. You may also wish to say each of the vocabulary words aloud and ask children to determine which two words rhyme with each other *(should, wood)*.

TARGET SKILL AND STRATEGY

DRAW CONCLUSIONS Model: On page 4, I read that the dad calls the animal shelter for help. I know that you shouldn't touch animals out in the wild. Based on this information and what I know, I think calling the animal shelter when you find an injured animal is the right thing to do. After children have read page 8, ask: Why do you think the owl is let go near a forest? *(it lives near there)*

BACKGROUND KNOWLEDGE Remind children that when they read, it helps to think about what they already know. What they already know can be from experiences they've had, from reading, or from things other people have taught them. Ask: What did you already know about owls before you read this story? How did it help you understand the story better?

ELL To support greater comprehension, invite children to retell the story in their native languages.

ADDITIONAL SKILL INSTRUCTION

CAUSE AND EFFECT Help children understand *cause*-and-*effect* relationships by discussing what happened (effect) in the story and why it happened (cause). Ask: What happens at the beginning of the story? *(The boy finds the owl in his yard.)* Why was the owl in the yard? *(It was hurt.)* Continue in the same manner, discussing other events in the story and why they happened.

Name _____

Draw Conclusions

Use details from the story *Fly Away Owl!* and what you already to answer the questions. Circle your answer.

I. How does the boy know the owl is hurt?

it can't fly   it is in his yard

2. How did the woman from the animal shelter know the owl's wing was broken?

she knows a lot about animals   the owl was hopping

3. Why did many weeks pass before the owl could fly?

it did not want to   it takes a long time to heal

4. How does the boy feel at the end of the story?

sad to see the owl go   happy the owl is better

Draw a picture of where the owl might live.

Name _____

Vocabulary

Practice writing each of the vocabulary words twice on the lines below.

door _____   _____

loved _____   _____

should _____   _____

wood _____   _____

Complete each sentence with the correct vocabulary word.

1. The boy found the owl near some _____ in his yard.

2. Dad opened the _____ when the boy yelled.

3. Dad knew that they _____ call the animal shelter.

4. The boy _____ watching the owl fly away.

What a Detective Does

SUMMARY This nonfiction reader describes what detectives do. It supports the lesson concept that detectives need great ideas and good powers of observation to solve mysteries.

LESSON VOCABULARY

among	another
instead	none

INTRODUCE THE BOOK

INTRODUCE THE TITLE AND AUTHOR Discuss with children the title and the author of *What a Detective Does*. Based on the title, ask children what kind of information they think this book will provide. Ask: Have you ever seen police officers asking people questions? Why do you think they were asking questions?

BUILD BACKGROUND Discuss detectives with children. Ask: Have you ever had to solve a mystery before? Maybe you had to find out who in your house ate the last cookie. How did you solve the mystery?

PREVIEW/TAKE A PICTURE WALK Have children look at the illustrations in the book. Ask: What do you think is going to happen in the book? On page 6, ask: What is being held in the boy's hand? Do you know what a magnifying glass is? What does it do? Who uses that kind of tool and why?

ELL Have children look at the illustrations. Point to the blender and toaster on page 3 and have children provide the English word. Ask: What is wrong with the cookie jar on page 4? Point to the magnifying glass on page 6, and give them the word for the object if they do not know it. Then have children say in English what some of the objects do. For example, "A toaster makes toast," "A blender mixes ingredients," and "A magnifying glass makes objects bigger."

READ THE BOOK

SET PURPOSE Have children set a purpose for their reading. Draw their attention to the illustrations. Ask: What do you want to know about the book?

STRATEGY SUPPORT: MONITOR AND CLARIFY Remind children that as good readers read, they *monitor* their understanding and *clarify* misunderstandings. Explain that sometimes you have to ask your peers for help. Have children sit in a circle and take turns reading each page. At the end of every page, ask children if they have any questions. Then have the other children answer each child's question.

COMPREHENSION QUESTIONS

PAGE 5 What does a detective do? *(solves mysteries by figuring out what happened)*

PAGE 4 How do you know that the dog did not break the cookie jar? *(The paw prints are too small.)*

PAGE 6 What is a clue? *(It helps tell you what happened.)*

PAGE 7 If you cannot find a clue, what else can you do to solve a mystery? *(You can ask people questions.)*

REVISIT THE BOOK

THINK AND SHARE

1. Detectives and scientists both look for clues and ask questions. A scientist works in a lab.
2. Possible response: I can reread a page if I don't understand something.
3. Possible responses: *cookie, book, took*
4. Possible response: There could be footprints instead of paw prints. The jar probably would have broken from falling on the floor, not by being tipped over.

EXTEND UNDERSTANDING After reading, have children go back and look at the illustrations. Ask, How does each illustration help you understand what is happening in the text?

RESPONSE OPTIONS

WRITING Have children pick out four illustrations. Then have them write one sentence about each illustration using their vocabulary words.

WORD WORK Have children make flash cards with the vocabulary word on one side and the definition on the other. Pair children up and have them quiz each other on the vocabulary.

SCIENCE CONNECTION

Discuss the five senses and which body organs provide each sense. Then have children act out a mystery scene in which the sense is important. Guide their activity by suggesting various events for each sense, for example, hearing a lost cat mewing in a tree or smelling perfume to know who is hiding in the dark.

Skill Work

TEACH/REVIEW VOCABULARY

Review vocabulary words with children. Write the words on the chalkboard, then ask children to pick out the words that have the same sound for the letter *o*. (*among, another, none*) Have children pick out other words in the reader with the /uh/ sound for the letter *o* (*someone, sometimes, some*).

TARGET SKILL AND STRATEGY

COMPARE AND CONTRAST Tell children that when you *compare* two things, you tell how they are alike. When you *contrast* two things, you tell how they are different. Good readers compare and contrast information as they read to better understand the information. Have children compare the facial expressions on Grandma, the boy, and the animals on page 3. Ask: How does this lead to a clue?

MONITOR AND CLARIFY Explain that good readers know that reading has to make sense and are aware when the text no longer makes sense to them. This is *monitoring*. When children do not understand something, they should use *clarifying* strategies to help their understanding. Have children reread text to find answers to their questions. Remind children that if they review what they have read, it will help them understand how things are alike or different.

ADDITIONAL SKILL INSTRUCTION

CAUSE AND EFFECT Use the terms "what happened" and "why it happened" to discuss *cause* and *effect*. Model for children: "'I shared my lunch with my friend, *so* my friend was happy.' What happened is 'my friend was happy.' Why it happened is 'I shared my lunch.'" Ask: What happened on page 3? Why did it happen? Rephrase the answer and write it on the chalkboard: *The jar broke <u>because</u> the cat knocked it over.* Explain that in this sentence *because* is a clue word that points to why something happened.

Name _____

Compare and Contrast

Use what you read on page 8 of *What a Detective Does* to fill in the diagram below.

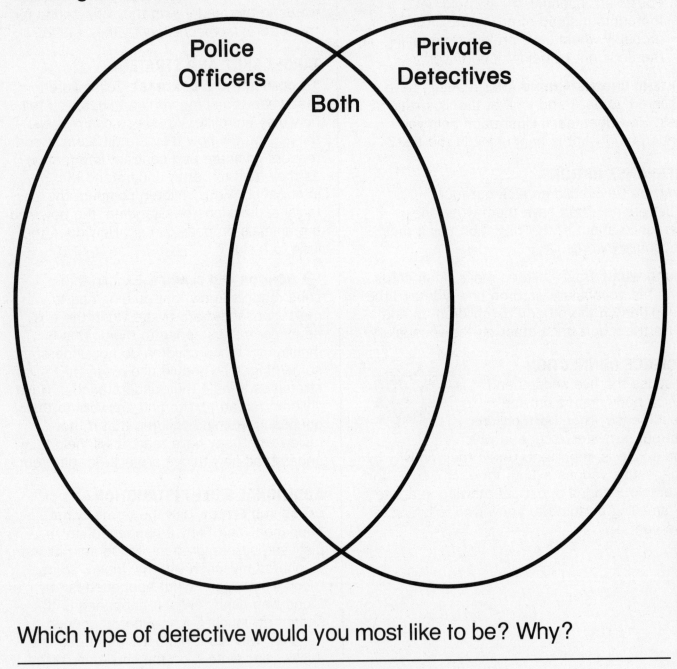

Police
Officers

Private
Detectives

Both

Which type of detective would you most like to be? Why?

_____

_____

_____

_____

Name _____

Vocabulary

Write the word or words that best fit each sentence.

Words to Know
among   another   instead   none

_____

1. The cat sat _____ the cookie crumbs and broken pieces of the jar.

_____

2. Joe wanted to eat _____ cookie.

_____

3. Grandma ate _____ of the cookies.

_____

4. We knew the cat broke the jar _____ of the dog.

5. Use the word *instead* in a sentence.

_____

_____

_____

_____

_____

The Inclined Plane

SUMMARY This selection describes inclined planes as simple machines that make it easier to move objects and people. Pictures and text examine many different kinds of inclined planes, such as ramps, slides, and hills.

LESSON VOCABULARY

against	goes
heavy	kinds
today	

INTRODUCE THE BOOK

INTRODUCE THE TITLE AND AUTHOR Discuss with children the title and author of *The Inclined Plane*. Draw children's attention to the content triangle on the cover. Ask: What other books about science have you read? How do you think this book will relate to science?

BUILD BACKGROUND Remind children that a plane is a flat surface. Then ask them to discuss the various inclined planes they may have used, such as slides on the playground, a hill for winter sledding, or a wheelchair ramp. If possible, show pictures from the Internet or reference books of inclined planes used in the construction of cathedrals and other large buildings or monuments.

PREVIEW/TAKE A PICTURE WALK Have children read the title and spend a few minutes looking at the illustrations and photos. Discuss what these suggest about the selection's content. Look, for example, at the picture on page 8 of the boy lifting the box straight up. Ask: What does his expression tell us about lifting the box? Draw children's attention to the pyramid worker on page 12 and ask: What does this tell us about the history of inclined planes?

READ THE BOOK

SET PURPOSE Guide children to set their own purposes for reading the selection. Children's interest in simple machines or physical activities should guide this purpose. Suggest that children imagine times when they have used simple or complex machines to do something.

STRATEGY SUPPORT: SUMMARIZE As children read, extracting the main ideas for the purpose of summarizing will help them understand and retain what they read. Help young children learn to summarize by suggesting that they retell in their own words as much of the selection as they recall. As an aid, if necessary, draw up a list for children to see of the types of inclined planes mentioned in this selection.

COMPREHENSION QUESTIONS

PAGE 3 Read the second paragraph on page 3. What is the paragraph's most important sentence? *(All that moving is a lot of work!)*

PAGE 5 What are two important details about an inclined plane? *(Possible responses: It's higher on one end and it has a flat surface.)*

PAGE 9 What does the picture tell you about moving things up an inclined plane? *(The boy's expression is happy, so it must be easy to move the box.)*

PAGE 10 How might you use an inclined plane today? *(Responses will vary.)*

REVISIT THE BOOK

THINK AND SHARE

1. Possible response: *All About Inclined Planes*
2. Possible response: Inclined planes are simple machines that make work easier to do.
3. Responses will vary.
4. Possible responses may decribe playground slides, exit ramps, or airport ramps.

EXTEND UNDERSTANDING Go over the photos and pictures in the selection. Ask children to note what the pictures have in common. Guide children to use the pictures in drawing up a description of the essential features of all inclined planes. Ask: What do these pictures tell you that you don't learn from the words?

RESPONSE OPTIONS

VIEWING Bring in or have children bring in examples from books, magazines, or the Internet of many different kinds of inclined planes. Include pictures of inclined planes used in different historical eras, such as ramps used to build medieval fortresses or modern bridges or scaffolding.

SCIENCE CONNECTION

Have children perform a simple experiment by lifting a weight from the floor to shoulder height. Be mindful of safety. Then have children push the same weight up a ramp or slide. Ask them to observe which action required more effort.

Skill Work

TEACH/REVIEW VOCABULARY

Reinforce comprehension by helping children to make a word web around each vocabulary word. Place the vocabulary word at the center of the web. Place all associated words in circles around the main word. Repeat this exercise for each of the vocabulary words.

ELL Distribute clues to the vocabulary words on cards and invite children to identify the word to which each clue refers. Use synonyms, antonyms, phrases, or idioms as clues.

TARGET SKILL AND STRATEGY

MAIN IDEA Tell children that a *main idea* is what an article is all about. The main idea gives the gist of a selection. Guide students in identifying the main idea of *The Inclined Plane* by asking: What do you see on every page of this article? For first graders, a phrase such as *inclined planes* can adequately express the main idea.

SUMMARIZE Explain to children that a summary of an article is a brief statement that gives the main idea and leaves out unimportant details. Invite children to recall the important ideas of the article and restate them in their own words.

ADDITIONAL SKILL INSTRUCTION

CAUSE AND EFFECT Tell children that a *cause* is why something happens, and an *effect* is what happens. Give an example: "Using a ramp to move a box is a cause; the effect is that it is easier to move the box." Focusing on simple machines or physical activities, invite children to think of other cause-and-effect relationships. Point out that sometimes one cause may have more than one effect.

Name _____

Main Idea

A **main idea** is the most important idea about a passage or group of sentences.

Read the sentences below.

> Some people have jobs where they have to move heavy things. Movers move boxes. Builders move things when they build. Drivers move things with their trucks. All that moving is a lot of work!

I. What are the sentences all about? Circle the correct answer.

a. moving things

b. building things

c. playing with trucks

d. having work

Directions Read the sentences below and then fill in the blank line with a title based on the Main Idea.

> You can use an inclined plane to do all kinds of things. You could use it to slide a box up a ramp. You could use it to push a wheelbarrow up a hill. You could also use it to go down a water slide!

2. _____

Name _____

Vocabulary

Directions Pick a word from the box to finish each sentence. Write it on the line.

Words to Know
against   goes   heavy   kinds   today

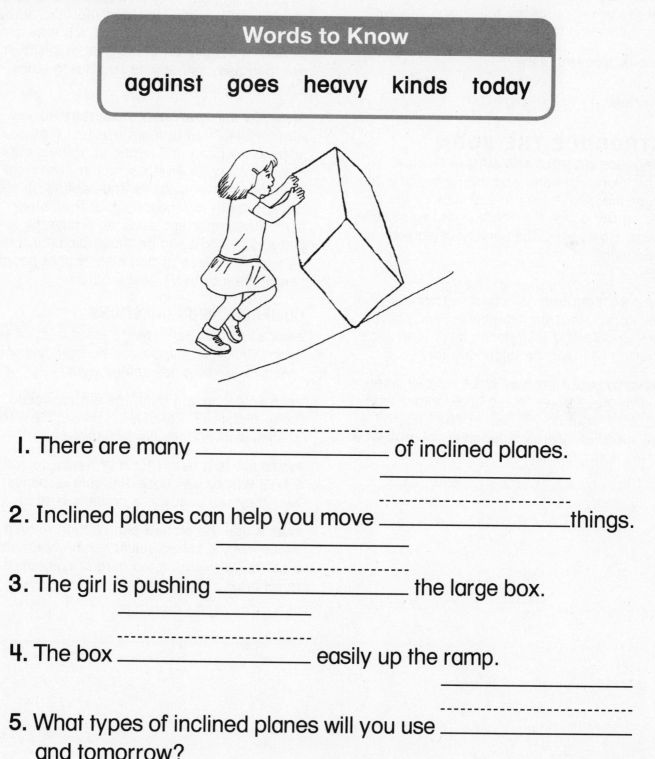

1. There are many _____ of inclined planes.

2. Inclined planes can help you move _____ things.

3. The girl is pushing _____ the large box.

4. The box _____ easily up the ramp.

5. What types of inclined planes will you use _____ and tomorrow?

Using the Telephone

SUMMARY This book presents information on the invention of the telephone and how it is used today. It supports the lesson concept that the invention of the telephone improved communication in our world.

LESSON VOCABULARY

built	early	learn
science	through	

INTRODUCE THE BOOK

INTRODUCE THE TITLE AND AUTHOR Discuss with children the title and author of *Using the Telephone*. Also have children look at the picture on the cover. Say: Scientists invent new things. How might this book have something to do with science?

BUILD BACKGROUND Ask children to share what they know about the telephone. Ask: Do you think people had telephones long, long ago? What do you use the telephone for?

PREVIEW/TAKE A PICTURE WALK Have children look at the pictures in the book before reading. Ask: What do you see in every photo? Why are there words below every photo? What is this book about?

READ THE BOOK

SET PURPOSE Have children set a purpose for reading *Using the Telephone*. Remind children of what they discussed when the title, author, and cover art were introduced. You may need to work with children to have them set their own purpose. Ask: Would you like to learn about using a telephone?

STRATEGY SUPPORT: TEXT STRUCTURE Review with children that authors use text features, such as pictures and captions, to help organize the story, or give it structure. Have children look at the pictures and caption on page 5. Lead them to recognize that the author illustrates important ideas on a page by using pictures. Say: Based on these pictures, I think an important idea of this page is that people use phones to talk to each other.

COMPREHENSION QUESTIONS

PAGE 3 Why did Bell have to learn a lot of science? *(Possible response: Science helps you invent by learning how things work.)*

PAGE 4 Why do you think the author used these pictures? *(Possible response: He wanted to show how phones have changed.)*

PAGES 6–7 Is it better for a grown-up to call 9-1-1? Why or why not? *(Possible response: Yes. They can describe a problem better.)*

PAGE 8 Use the picture and caption to help you explain why a school might not be open after a storm. *(It might be too hard or dangerous to travel after a heavy snow.)*

REVISIT THE BOOK

THINK AND SHARE

1. Possible response: First: the history of the telephone; Next: how phones work; Last: why phones are useful.
2. 1: Dial 9-1-1; 2: Tell the problem; 3: Stay on the line.
3. Possible response: *jaw, law, paw*
4. Possible response: It makes it easier to contact people.

EXTEND UNDERSTANDING Point out the simple photo diagram on page 7. Ask: What do the circles tell you? Why is there a finger in the picture?

RESPONSE OPTIONS

WRITING Have children write one or two sentences telling why they liked or did not like this book.

SCIENCE CONNECTION

Display books and other information about 19th-century inventions. Have children choose one invention. Then, ask them to write a sentence about how to use the invention.

Skill Work

TEACH/REVIEW VOCABULARY

Give pairs of children a set of vocabulary word cards. Give them another set with these clues, but first read them aloud: I went to bed before my bedtime. You learn this at school. You do this with a teacher. To enter, you must go ____. This house was ____ by Jack. Have pairs play a memory game by revealing each vocabulary word and its clue.

ELL Use the same cards for this activity. Pair children with more-proficient speakers who will read and act out clues. The non-native English speaker will say and show the correct vocabulary word.

TARGET SKILL AND STRATEGY

SEQUENCE Remind children that *sequence* is the order in which things happen. Have children look at the text and picture on page 3. Ask: What date is listed on this page? *(1876)* Explain to children that this is a long time ago. Have children look at the pictures on page 5. Say: These are the kinds of phones we use today. This tells me that the sequence we are learning about phones is from the oldest to the newest.

TEXT STRUCTURE Explain to children that authors can organize their stories a number of ways. One of these ways is by topics. Ask children what the first part of *Using the Telephone* is about. *(the history of the telephone; how telephones work)* Ask: What is the second part about? *(why telephones are useful)*

ADDITIONAL SKILL INSTRUCTION

AUTHOR'S PURPOSE As you preview the book with the children, ask: What do you think the book will be like—funny, sad, serious, exciting? During reading, ask follow-up questions, such as: Were you right about what the book is about? Also ask supporting questions as children analyze the author's purpose, such as: What part of this book seemed serious?

Name _____

Sequence

Use the boxes below to make a picture story of how phones have changed over time. Make sure your pictures show the oldest phone to the newest.

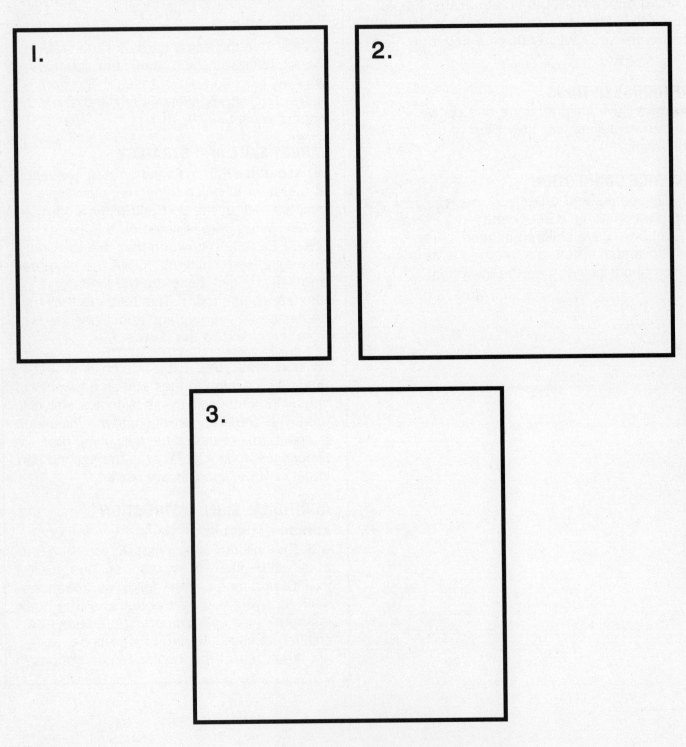

1.

2.

3.

Name _____

Vocabulary

Circle the picture that each word describes.

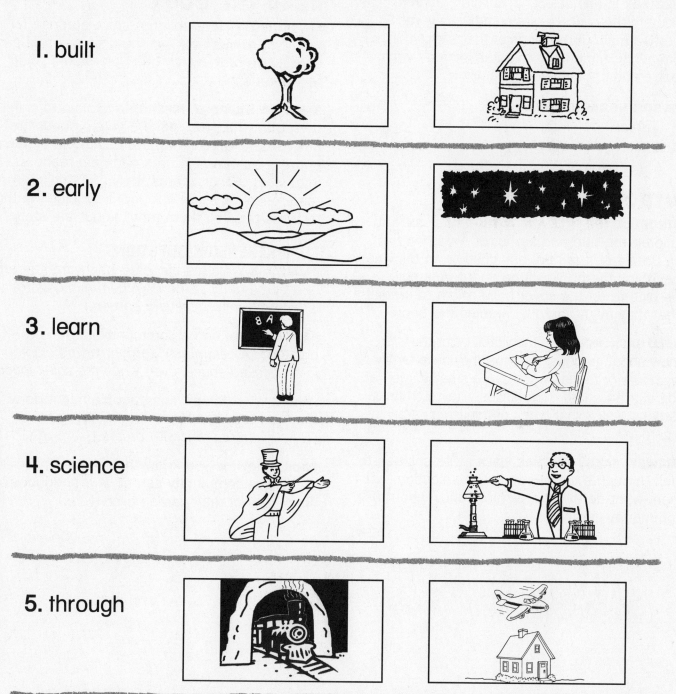

1. built

2. early

3. learn

4. science

5. through

A Garden for All

SUMMARY In this selection, children are introduced to the concept of a community garden. They learn about the types of things grown in a community garden and that it is shared by many people and not for just one family.

LESSON VOCABULARY

answer	carry
different	poor

INTRODUCE THE BOOK

INTRODUCE THE TITLE AND AUTHOR Discuss with children the title and author of *A Garden for All*. Based on the title, ask children to tell what they think the book will be about. Ask how the picture on the cover helps them to predict what they might learn by reading the book.

BUILD BACKGROUND Ask children what they know about gardens. Perhaps they have family members or friends who have a small garden at home or have had experiences with community gardens. Ask: What types of things can grow in a garden?

PREVIEW/TAKE A PICTURE WALK Invite children to look through the pictures in the selection. Ask them what details the pictures show about a community garden.

READ THE BOOK

SET PURPOSE Have children set a purpose for reading *A Garden for All*. The discussion of gardens while previewing the book should guide this purpose.

STRATEGY SUPPORT: INFERRING Explain to children that when you make a guess about the story or a character without being told by the author, you *infer*. Pictures can help readers infer what a character is feeling. As children read, encourage them to looks for clues in the pictures that tell them more about the story.

COMPREHENSION QUESTIONS

PAGES 4–5 Which is bigger, a backyard garden or a community garden? (*A community garden is bigger than a backyard garden.*)

PAGE 5 Where can a community garden be planted? (*A community garden can be planted in an unused space, even when the soil is poor.*)

PAGE 7 What is one thing people might do with the food they grow in a community garden? (*They might share it with others.*)

PAGE 8 How do you know that people think planting a community garden is a good idea? (*They replant their garden every year.*)

REVISIT THE BOOK

THINK AND SHARE

1. Community gardens are for many people. Gardens in yards are for a few people.
2. Possible response: I think people like working together. This helps me understand why so many people replant their gardens every year.
3. Possible response: *carry* tools, *water* plants, *dig, clean up*
4. Responses will vary.

EXTEND UNDERSTANDING Have children examine the illustrations. Ask: What do the illustrations on pages 6 and 7 show you about the kinds of things people do in a community garden? Guide children to see how illustrations add to their understanding of a selection.

RESPONSE OPTIONS

WORD WORK Review the prefixes *un-* and *re-* with the children. Have them look through the book for examples of these prefixes: *unused* on page 5 and *replant* and page 8. Ask them to think of other words that use these prefixes (for example, *untie, unpack, reuse,* and *rewrite*).

SCIENCE CONNECTION

Have children use the library or the Internet to research the types of flowers, fruits, and vegetables that would grow well in your area. Have them find or draw pictures of these plants and make a bulletin board showing "A Classroom Garden."

Skill Work

TEACH/REVIEW VOCABULARY

Have children find the word *different* in the selection. Invite them to use the word in a sentence of their own. Continue in a similar fashion with the other vocabulary words.

ELL Encourage English language learners to write and say the vocabulary words and think of how to say the words in their home languages. Give them a sentence using one of the words to read and repeat with you.

TARGET SKILL AND STRATEGY

THEME Share with children that the *theme* of a story is the "big idea" or the lesson that readers learn from the story. You might share with children other nonfiction books you have read and discuss its theme. Then encourage children to think about the theme of *A Garden for All*.

INFERRING Remind children that readers can infer things from the story by looking at the text and the pictures, and by using their own personal experiences. Have children read page 6 and look at the picture. Say: The story says that people carry tools, but it doesn't say what kind of tools. Are there any clues in the picture that tell us what kinds of tools people use to garden? (*Possible responses: hoe, rake, shovel*)

ADDITIONAL SKILL INSTRUCTION

SEQUENCE Remind children that sequence is what happens first, next, and last. Invite them to think about what happens first, next, and last in the book as they read. They may want to fill in a graphic organizer as they read to keep track of the sequence of events.

Name_____

Theme

Read the questions about *A Garden for All*.
Circle your answers.

1. What is the topic of this story?

yards   community gardens

_____

2. What is true about a community garden?

it is different from a yard   it takes very little work

_____

3. What can people grow in a community garden?

flowers   tools

_____

4. Use the pictures to infer the theme. What is the theme of this story?

A community garden is good for the community.

A community garden is different from a yard.

Name_____

Vocabulary

Read the sentences below. Fill in the blank with the correct vocabulary word.

Words to Know
answer   carry   different   poor

1. A community garden is _____ from a yard garden.

2. "I'll help you plant flowers," was Mother's _____.

3. Dad asked me to _____ vegetables to Mr. Bark's house.

4. A community garden can sometimes have _____ soil.

5. Write your own sentence using a word from the box.

_____

_____

_____

T-Chart

Suggestions You can use this chart to record information in two categories or for various sorting activities. Write the heading at the top of each column.

Three-Column Chart

Suggestions You can use this chart to record information in three categories or for various sorting activities. Write the heading at the top of each column.

Classify

 Suggestions Children can use this chart to classify information. For example, pictures of animals could be placed in the circle and then sorted into land animals and water animals in the boxes below.

Pictograph

Title _____

 Suggestions Help children make a pictograph to record information. Children draw simple pictures on the chart or on self-stick notes to represent each item. Record the topic at the top of the chart. Some possible topics are: *What did we have for lunch? What pets do we have? What color shoes are we wearing?*

Web A

 Suggestions You can use this chart to activate children's prior knowledge about a topic. Write a major concept in the circle such as *Pets* or *Machines.* Children write or dictate words or ideas that relate to the concept. Write them so that the lines connect them to the circle.

Web B

Suggestions You can use this chart to activate children's prior knowledge about a topic. Write a major concept in the middle circle, such as *Things at School*. In the smaller circles, children dictate words or ideas that relate to the concept. Additional ideas may be added on spokes coming from the smaller circles.

KWL Chart

K	W	L
What We Know	**What We Want to Know**	**What We Learned**

Suggestions Have children tell what they know or think they know about the topic. Record their responses in the column **What We Know.** Ask children what they would like to learn. List their questions in **What We Want to Know.** After children learn more about the topic, discuss what they learned. List children's responses in **What We Learned.**

Prediction

Suggestions You can use this chart to help children discuss predictions. Have children suggest what might happen next in a story or other situation. Children may draw a picture and dictate sentences to show the prediction.

Sequence

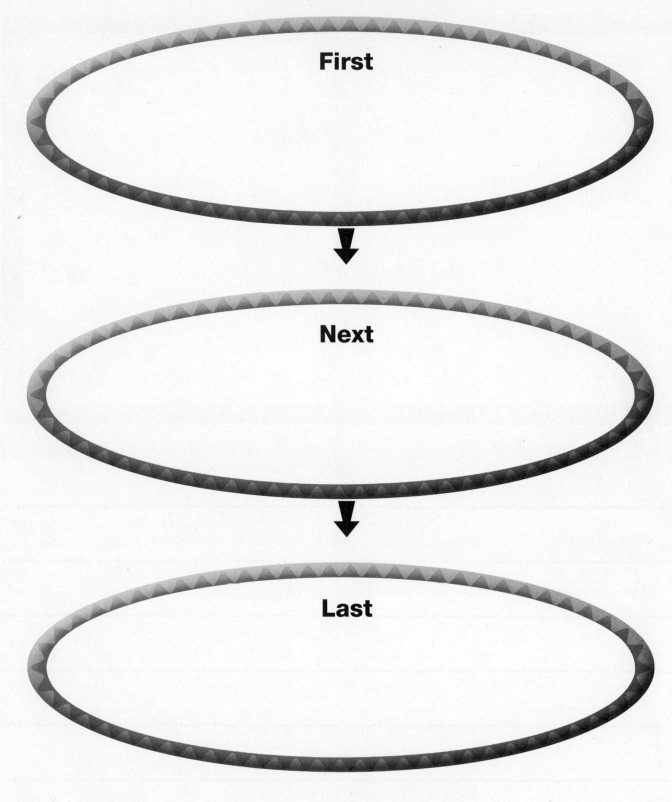

First

Next

Last

Suggestions Use this chart to help children place events in sequence. Children can draw pictures or dictate what happened first, next, and last.

Story Sequence A

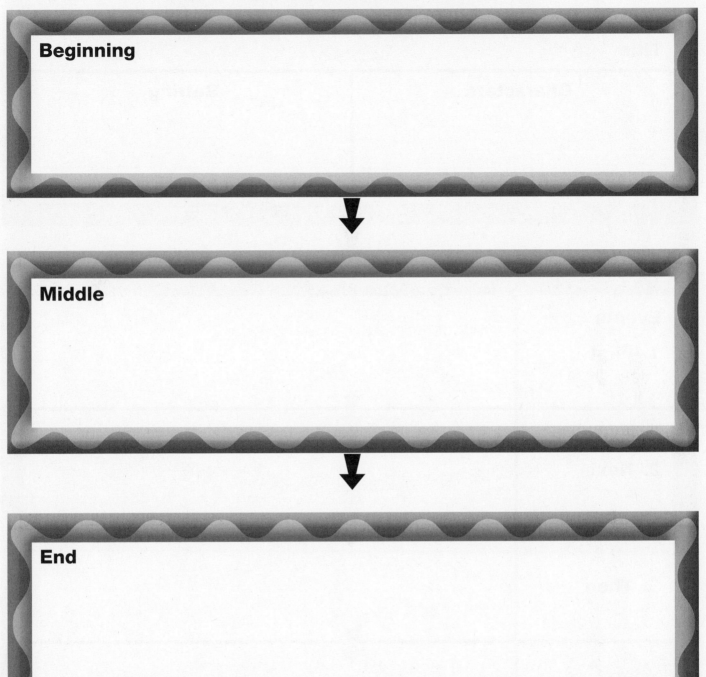

Beginning

Middle

End

![apple] **Suggestions** Use this chart to help children place events in a story in sequence. Children can draw pictures or dictate what happened in the beginning, middle, and end.

Story Sequence B

Title

Characters	Setting

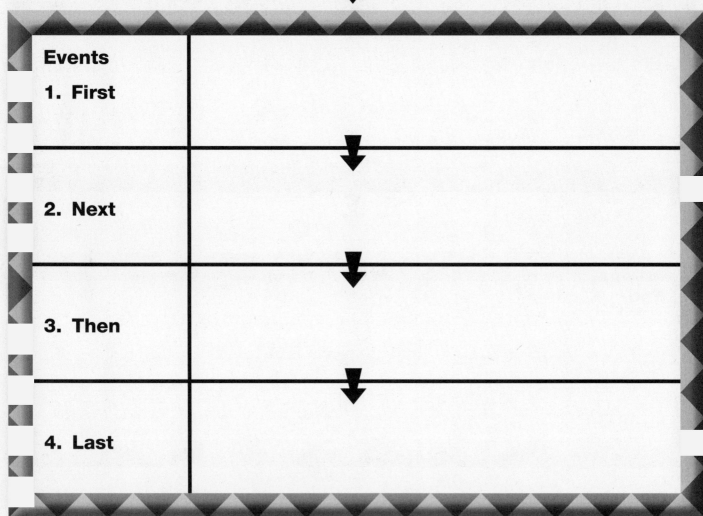

Events

1. First

2. Next

3. Then

4. Last

Suggestions After recording the title, characters, and setting of a story, children chart the sequence of events. This organizer helps children understand how one event leads to another.

Book Report

Title _____

Author _____

Illustrator _____

Setting _____

Characters _____

Our Favorite Parts _____

Suggestions You can use this chart to record information about a big book or trade book. Discuss where the story takes place, what happens in the book, and how children feel about the book. Invite children to draw pictures of their favorite parts of the book.

Story Comparison

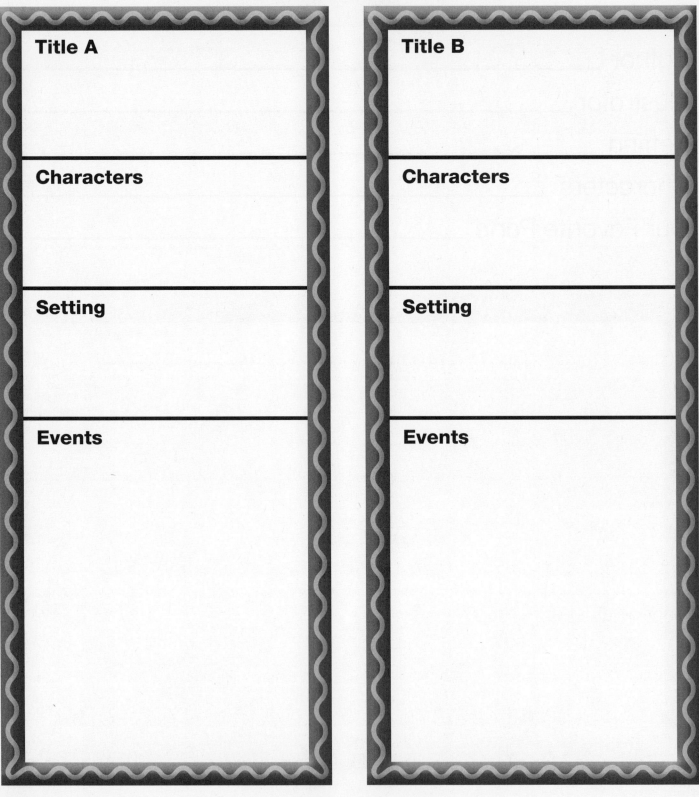

Title A

Characters

Setting

Events

Title B

Characters

Setting

Events

Suggestions Use this chart to help children compare story elements and structures. This type of activity prepares children for working with Venn diagrams. Children may illustrate or dictate these comparisons.

Question the Author

Title _____

Author _____ Page _____

1. What does the author tell you?	
2. Why do you think the author tells you that?	
3. Does the author say it clearly?	
4. What would make it clearer?	
5. How would you say it instead?	

Suggestions Use this chart to help children understand the author's purpose and the author's craft. Students analyze what was said, how well it was said, and how it might be said differently.

Main Idea

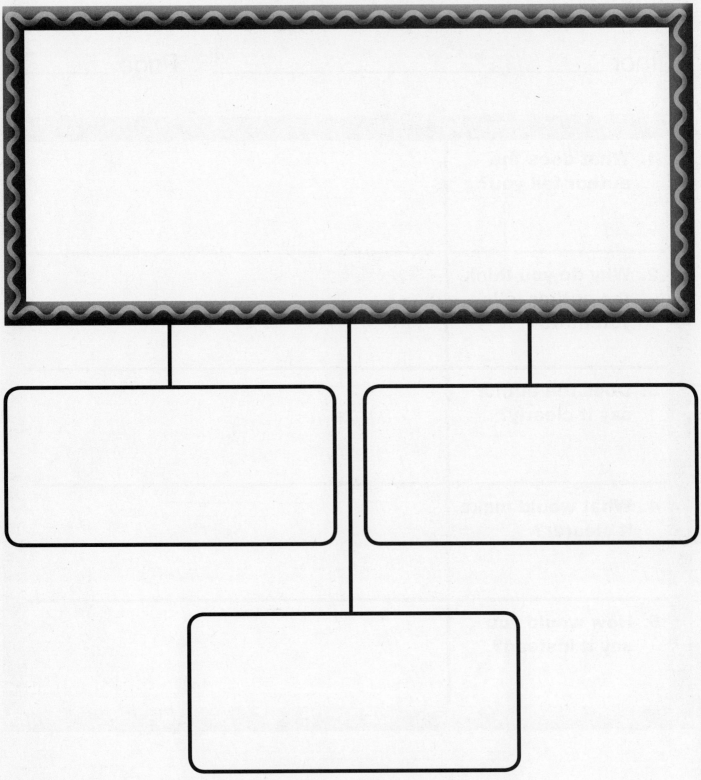

Suggestions Use this chart to help children understand the main idea of what they read. Ask: *What is the story all about?* Write children's responses in the top box. Have children draw or dictate in the smaller boxes other things they remember from the story.

Venn Diagram

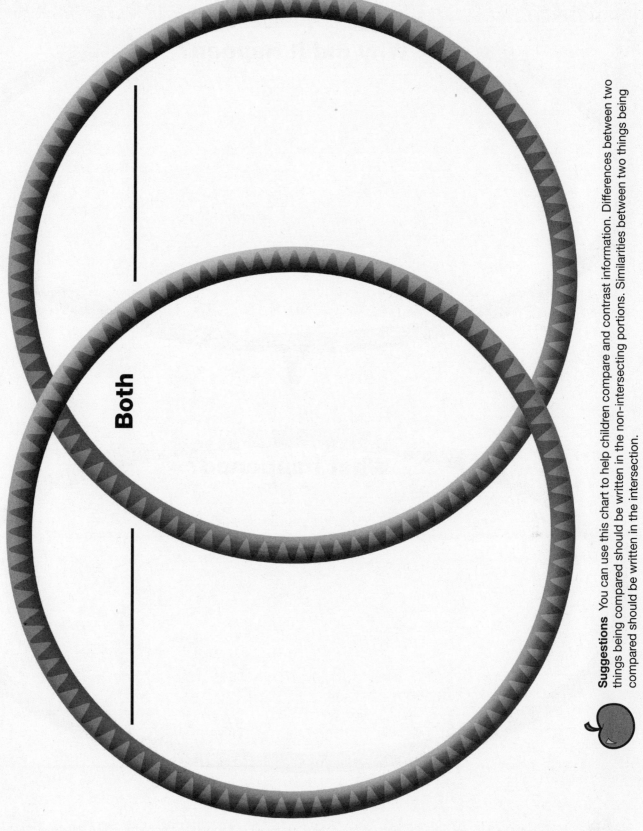

Both

Suggestions You can use this chart to help children compare and contrast information. Differences between two things being compared should be written in the non-intersecting portions. Similarities between two things being compared should be written in the intersection.

Cause and Effect

Why did it happen?

What happened?

Suggestions Use this chart to help children understand what happens (effect) and why it happens (cause). Children draw pictures in the appropriate ovals or dictate sentences to show an event. Help children think back and describe or draw what caused that event to happen.

Cycle Chart

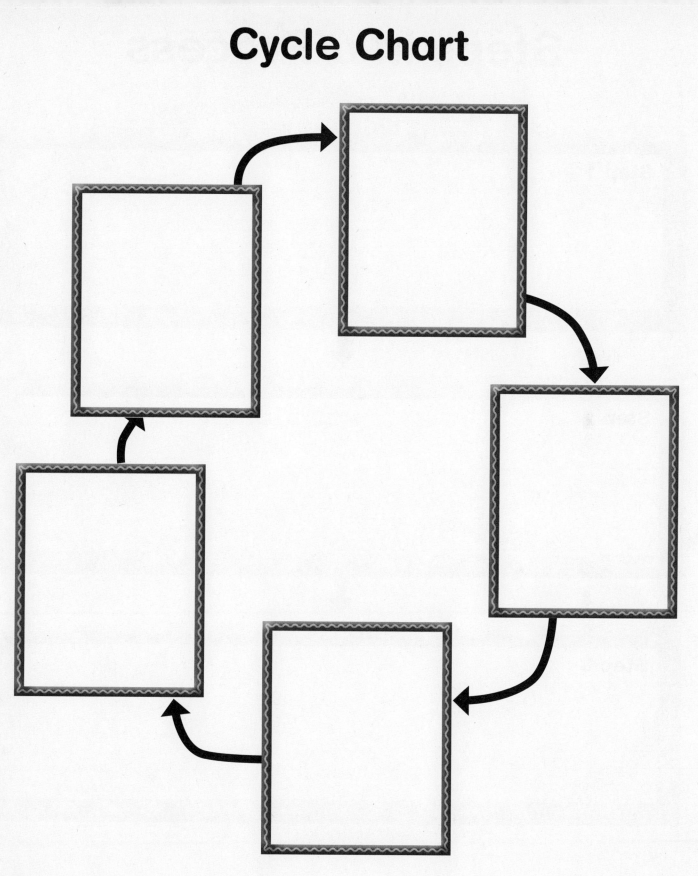

Suggestions Use this chart to help children understand how a series of events produces a series of results again and again. Discuss such questions as: *How does one event lead to another? What is the final outcome?* This chart works well for depicting life cycles.

Steps in a Process

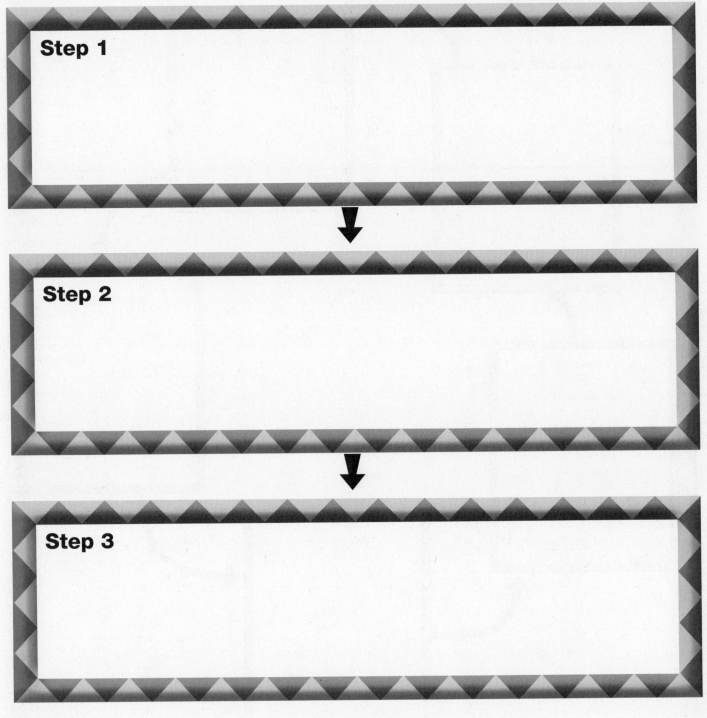

Step 1

Step 2

Step 3

Suggestions Use this chart to help children break down a process. This chart works well with a how-to activity that has a few simple steps. Students may draw pictures or dictate how to do something.

Writing Topics

Family	Friends	Pets

Hobbies	Favorite Activities

Special Places	Favorite Vacations

Happy Times	Times I Felt Proud

Suggestions Use this chart as a writing resource or interest inventory. Over time, children can generate numerous topics for future compositions.

Letter Format

_____

_____

Dear _____,

_____

_____

_____

_____

_____

_____

_____

_____

----------------------------------,

_____

_____

Suggestions Use this organizer to help children understand the format of a letter. The format can be used for writing to friends, family, or characters from a story.